# Israel
# Democracy or Apartheid State?

# ISRAEL
## DEMOCRACY OR
## APARTHEID
## STATE?

## by Josh Ruebner

OLIVE
BRANCH
PRESS

An imprint of Interlink Publishing Group, Inc.
www.interlinkbooks.com

First published in 2018 by

Olive Branch Press
An imprint of Interlink Publishing Group, Inc.
46 Crosby Street, Northampton, MA 01060
www.interlinkbooks.com

Library of Congress Cataloging-in-Publication Data
Names: Ruebner, Josh, author.
Title: Israel : democracy or apartheid state? / by Josh Ruebner.
Description: Northampton, MA : Olive Branch Press, an imprint of Interlink
    Publishing Group, Inc., 2017.
Identifiers: LCCN 2017031227 | ISBN 9781566560290
Subjects: LCSH: Palestinian Arabs—Politics and government. | Arab-Israeli
    conflict. | Israel--Politics and government. | Democracy—Israel. |
    Zionism.
Classification: LCC DS119.7 .R764 2017 | DDC 956.9405--dc23
LC record available at https://lccn.loc.gov/2017031227

Cover image: Sculptural Assemblage © Rajie Cook, 2009

Printed and bound in the United States of America

To request our free 48-page, full-color catalog, write to us at
Interlink Publishing, 46 Crosby Street, Northampton, Massachusetts 01060,
call us toll-free at 1-800-238-LINK, or visit our website at www.interlinkbooks.com

*For Rami,*
*May you grow up in a world in which*
*everyone enjoys freedom, justice and equality.*

# CONTENTS

Palestinian homes remain standing in the village of Lifta.

# Skinny-dipping in Lifta

Travel west out of Jerusalem on the main highway to Tel Aviv, turn left on Begin Boulevard, go past the Golda Meir Interchange and follow the sign to Mey Neftoah to see one of the most extraordinary sights in Israel, one not likely to be found in your travel guide. In parentheses, the sign hints at what you will encounter: Lifta, a once-prosperous Palestinian village depopulated in December 1947 after a Zionist militia raided the village's coffee house, killing five civilians and causing many of the rest to flee.

What makes this Palestinian village unique among the more than 500 villages depopulated by Zionist militias and the State of Israel before, during and after Israel's establishment in 1948 is the fact that some of its houses remain intact. Lifta is the only depopulated Palestinian village not completely bulldozed or repopulated with Israeli Jews.

Dozens of Lifta's houses remain standing today, not because Israel wished to leave a reminder of its ethnic cleansing but because of a geological quirk: much of the village sits on a steep slope which is impenetrable to bulldozers.

On a cloudless, scorching day in June 2013, I visited Lifta on a guided tour led by a member of the Israeli organization Zochrot, which educates Israeli Jews about depopulated Palestinian villages.

Winding our way carefully down the sharp slopes of the hills to the valley's floor, we came upon the village's central water pool. On that day, a group of Russian immigrants cooled off by skinny-dipping, boisterously enjoying themselves with the aid of bottles of vodka.

They seemed blissfully oblivious to the history of the place, and who can blame them? No historical marker proclaims the previous existence of a Palestinian village there.

The concrete and partially visible rebar on some of the houses are an obvious testament to the modernity of these dwellings. I asked our tour guide what Israelis think of the provenance of these homes. She deadpanned that most, if they give it a second thought, assume that they are antiquities dating back to the rule of the Roman Empire two millennia ago.

Today the homes are used by Israeli drug addicts who get high under the cover of darkness. Hebrew graffiti is scrawled on the walls, and mounds of soot testify to the fires lit there to keep warm in the often damp, frigid Jerusalem evenings.

Beside the path through the village, I spotted some subversive Arabic graffiti etched into the leaf of a prickly pear cactus. *Aidoun*, it read. "Returning." Known in Arabic as *sabr*, which also translates into "patience," the prickly pear cactus has come to symbolize Palestinian determination to return to the lands from which they were expelled.

Understanding Israel today, the seemingly intractable issues which divide it from Palestinians, the fragility of its identity and its obsessive, almost frantic, demand to be recognized by others—to have its existence legitimated—is possible only by examining how this state was built upon and is maintained today on the destruction and subjugation of Palestinian society.

## Sources:

Anan Odeh, "Photostory: As long as there is life, there is hope," *Electronic Intifada*, January 20, 2008, available at:
https://electronicintifada.net/content/
photostory-long-there-life-there-hope/7306

# Israel Today:
# Between Normality and Incongruity

If Israeli Jews aspire to one thing above even security, it is this: normality. It is the desire to live an innocuous life, to be defined and perceived beyond the terms of Israel's relations to the Palestinians. It is why Israeli Prime Minister Benjamin Netanyahu took time out of his 2015 speech to the UN General Assembly, otherwise devoted to opposing the nuclear deal with Iran, to claim that Israel has "perfected" the cherry tomato. The sense of needing to be known—and accepted by the world—for something other than warfare and military occupation is palpable.

And in the quintessentially Israeli city of Tel Aviv, a booming metropolis situated along the shimmering Mediterranean Sea, a cosmopolitan city of gleaming skyscrapers and vast disparities between the elites and the have-nots, one can be forgiven for having the feeling of being transported to Miami or Los Angeles. While gamboling around the city, indulging in a latte in an outdoor café, sampling the latest internationally award-winning fusion restaurant, or taking in the vibrant arts scene, one can indeed temporarily flee the strictures and confines of the abnormality of modern-day Israel.

But the escapism is fleeting, ephemeral. Israel can contain Palestinians behind fences and walls. They can be out of sight, out of mind for the average Israeli. But the ineluctable presence and reality of the Palestinians intrudes into this artificial bubble, bursts its frivolity in ways both subtle and acute. From the security guard inspecting your backpack as you enter the mall, to the public bomb shelters lining the streets, to the bikinied woman on the beach with a machine gun strapped across her back, Israel's aspirations to normality are stymied. Israeli Jews often euphemistically and abstractly refer the unavoidable reality of their abnormal relationship with the Palestinians as *hamatzav*, "the situation" in English. *Hamatzav* regularly rears its head, no matter how forcefully Israeli Jews try to bury it underground.

Today the Tel Aviv district of Israel, which includes the neighboring city of Jaffa, boasts 1.35 million inhabitants. Founded in 1909 by some of the earliest Zionist colonists who immigrated to Palestine, Tel Aviv was designed to be the physical embodiment of Theodore Herzl's vision for an "Old New Land"—the manifestation of a modern Jewish city in the ancestral land of the Jewish people. This interplay between history and modernity is reflected in the city's name: *tel* is the Hebrew word for an archaeological mound and *aviv* is spring.

However, the founding of Tel Aviv was neither sui generis nor built upon an exclusive Jewish history. Like most of Israel today, Tel Aviv was constructed upon the ruins of Palestinian society, upon villages and towns that were depopulated and razed to create the Jewish state in 1948. Today Tel Aviv encompasses former Palestinian villages such as al-Manshiyya, a once thriving neighborhood of 12,000 people with 20 cafes, 14 carpentry shops, 12 bakeries, four schools and two mosques. Norma Musih, an Israeli Jewish editor of a guidebook on demolished Palestinian villages, told the Israeli newspaper *Haaretz* that she contributed to the iconoclastic book for the sake of her daughter. "I want her to know that here in Tel Aviv, by the sea that she loves so much, there was once a neighborhood in which children like herself lived, people who had full lives, desires, hatreds, loves and dreams," Musih said. "I want to tell her, without burdening her with the terror of the expulsion and the destruction."

Although vestiges of a Palestinian past in Tel Aviv are nearly all paved over today, they are irrefutable in Jaffa, immediately to the south. Jaffa was a bustling, culturally vibrant, wealthy Palestinian city in the nineteenth and first half of the twentieth century, a prototypical entrepôt with far-flung mercantile relations throughout the Mediterranean and beyond. This idyll was shattered when Zionist

**Corrugated tin mostly conceals Israel's desecration of the Muslim cemetery of Mamilla to build a Museum of Tolerance.**

militias laid siege to the city in March 1948; it fell on the same day that Israel was established two months later. Zionist militias displaced an estimated 95 percent of the population; the estimated 4,000 Palestinian residents who managed to resist this onslaught were "rounded up and ghettoized in al-Ajami neighborhood which was sealed off from the rest of the city and administered as essentially a military prison for two subsequent years," according to Sami Abu Shehadeh and Fadi Shbaytah of the Jaffa Popular Committee for the Defense of Land and Housing Rights.

Today Jaffa's Palestinian population is being subjected to the twin pressures of gentrification and Jewish exclusivism. In 2010, Israel's Supreme Court authorized a group of religious settlers from the West Bank to build Jewish-only segregated housing in the center of al-Ajami, which precipitated groups of young Israeli Jews to parade through the streets of Jaffa carrying out "miniature pogroms" against Palestinians, according to journalist Max Blumenthal, in which they yelled "Yafo [Hebrew for Jaffa] is just for Jews." This attempted takeover of al-Ajami reflects the inevitable tensions and incongruities between Israel's self-defined character as a Jewish state and its pretensions to democracy.

If Tel Aviv is Israel's young bon vivant then Jerusalem is its counterpoint: sober and heavily laden with the burden of millennia of religious and historical baggage. Ostensibly Israel's "eternal and undivided capital," Jerusalem today is deeply divided despite Israel's half-century of control over the whole city. A new light rail system gives the city a veneer of modernity, incongruously connecting Israel's illegal settlements in the eastern part of the city to Palestinian refugee camps to the pedestrian mall of Jaffa Street in the city's western half. Designed to integrate these settlements into the fabric of the city, the light rail has had unintended consequences: it has emboldened young Palestinians to leave the confines of their neighborhoods neglected by the municipality and bereft of amenities to venture into the western part of the city seeking amusement and a respite from military occupation. This integration has prompted a backlash. An anti-miscegenation group—Lehava (a Hebrew acronym for Prevention of Assimilation in the Holy Land)—regularly flyers the area with ominous warnings of Jewish girls being seduced by menacing Palestinians. And at the slightest outbreak of communal tensions, Israeli Jews roam the streets in lynch mob fashion seeking out Palestinian victims.

The Kafkaesque nature of today's Israel reaches the pinnacle of absurdity only a few blocks from Jaffa Street in Jerusalem. In view of an outdoor mall featuring the fashions of Tommy Hilfiger, The North Face, Guess and many other stores typically found in high-end shopping areas in the United States lies Mamilla Cemetery. This Muslim burial ground dates to the seventh century and is believed to house the remains of some of the Prophet Muhammad's companions. It is also the repose of soldiers from the eleventh century who fought with Salah ad-Din (known as Saladin in English) to drive out the Crusaders from Jerusalem. The historical and religious significance of the cemetery made it a coveted burial place for Jerusalem's

Palestinian notables, with prominent families such as the Husseinis, Dajanis and Khalidis laying to rest their ancestors there.

In 2011, the Israeli Interior Ministry gave permission to the Los Angeles-based organization The Simon Wiesenthal Center to build a "Museum of Tolerance" on a large portion of the Mamilla Cemetery. Israel fenced off a football field-sized tract of the cemetery with sheets of tall corrugated tin to prevent onlookers from witnessing the spectacle of bulldozers chewing up graves and disinterring bodies in a macabre and ironic paean to multiculturalism and the fight against racism and discrimination. To add insult to injury, in August 2015, an Israeli café chain which serves alcohol opened shop on the cemetery's grounds, further desecrating the space in Muslims' eyes since alcohol is forbidden in Islam.

These attempts to erase the Mamilla Cemetery serve as a telling metaphor for Israel's frantic and systematic attempts to uproot the past, cleansing the land of its non-Jewish history to validate its affectations as an exclusivist Jewish state. Israel may well have the power to depopulate and change the names of former Palestinian villages such as Isdud to its biblical equivalent Ashdod, but it cannot compel Palestinian refugees and their descendants living in refugee camps just a few miles away in the Gaza Strip from abandoning their memory. *Hamatzav* will perpetuate itself insatiably, and Israeli Jews will strive in vain for the normality they seek until they recognize the chimerical nature of today's State of Israel, constructed over the ruins of a Palestinian society whose people's resiliency remains undimmed.

## Sources:

Statistical Abstract of Israel 2015, available at:
http://www.cbs.gov.il/reader/shnaton/templ_shnaton_e.
html?num_tab=st02_16x&CYear=2015

Gideon Levy, "Arab Villages, Bulldozed From Our Memory," *Haaretz*, August 31, 2012, available at:
http://www.haaretz.com/weekend/twilight-zone/
arab-villages-bulldozed-from-our-memory-1.461986

Sami Abu Shehadeh and Fadi Shbaytah, "Jaffa: from eminence to ethnic cleansing," *The Electronic Intifada*, February 26, 2009, available at: https://electronicintifada.net/content/jaffa-eminence-ethnic-cleansing/8088

Max Blumenthal, *Goliath: Life and Loathing in Greater Israel*, Nation Books, 2013.

Campaign to Preserve Mamilla Jerusalem Cemetery, available at: http://www.mamillacampaign.org/

Creede Newton, "Muslims in Jerusalem decry cafe built on cemetery," *Al Jazeera*, August 10, 2015, available at: http://www.aljazeera.com/news/2015/08/muslims-jerusalem-decry-cafe-built-cemetery-150809084649792.html

# Barenboim Plays Wagner

Israeli culture and the arts bear an indelible European imprint thanks to the countries of origin of most early Zionist immigrants to Palestine in the late nineteenth and early twentieth centuries. This predilection is perhaps best captured in Israel's national love affair with classical music. Though its total population is less than New York City's, Israel boasts at least eight major symphony and philharmonic orchestras.

The 2016 lineup for the Israel Philharmonic Orchestra featured selections from Beethoven, Vivaldi, Mozart, Tchaikovsky, Mahler, Rachmaninov and other famous composers. One composer not on the list is the nineteenth-century German composer Richard Wagner. In Wagner's originally pseudonymous 1850 diatribe "Judaism in Music," he posited that a malign Jewish mannerism of speaking was corrupting German music and culture. Not coincidentally, Wagner's music was a favorite of Adolf Hitler, and his music was often played at Nazi rallies.

Because of Wagner's anti-Semitism and his association with Nazism, Israeli orchestras have traditionally steered clear of his music. In December 2000, however, the Argentinian-born and Israeli-raised conductor Daniel Barenboim announced that he would conduct Wagner's opera *The Valkyrie* at Israel's national arts festival the following summer. A furor erupted. Barenboim countered that he had "the greatest compassion for Holocaust survivors and understand their terrible associations with Wagner's music…However, the question must be asked if any person has the right to deprive another who does not have these same associations of hearing Wagner's music."

Bowing to the pressure, however, Barenboim removed Wagner's piece from the performance. But when he was brought back on stage for an encore, he asked audience members if they would like to hear Wagner's music. An emotional half-hour debate ensued, with dozens of audience members walking out in protest against "concentration camp music." But most of the audience remained and gave Barenboim a standing ovation after he played a piece from Wagner's *Tristan and Isolde* opera.

## Sources:

"Orchestras and Opera Houses—Israel," Musical Chairs, available at: https://www.musicalchairs.info/israel/orchestras?sort=or

"The flagship series of the Philharmonic. 11 concerts from the best of the IPO's repertoire," Israel Philharmonic Orchestra, available at: http://www.ipo.co.il/eng/Series/Subscribers/telaviv/Series,367.aspx?

Daniel Barenboim, "As a Democratic State, Israel Should Allow Wagner to Be Played," *Los Angeles Times*, May 21, 2001, available at: http://www.digitalnpq.org/global_services/global%20viewpoint/05-21-01.html

Ewen MacAskill, "Barenboim stirs up Israeli storm by playing Wagner," *The Guardian*, July 9, 2001, available at: http://www.theguardian.com/world/2001/jul/09/ewenmacaskill

# Israel's Economy

In the early decades of Zionist colonization of Palestine and the initial years of the State of Israel's existence, a carefully cultivated mythology emerged of the bronzed, muscular pioneer tilling the soil, singing folk songs, and living out a socialist utopia on a collective known as a kibbutz. While this image skewed perceptions of the actual Zionist economy in the *yishuv*, as the pre-state Jewish community in Palestine was known (it was always overwhelmingly urban), and the Israeli economy in its early years, today this impression is ever more out-moded. In 2014, agriculture accounted for only 2.4 percent of the Israeli economy, and less than 2 percent of Israelis lived on a kibbutz. Most agricultural work today in Israel is likely to be done by guest workers from countries such as Thailand, who have largely replaced Palestinian day laborers who have mostly been shut out of their former jobs in the Israeli agricultural sector since Israel began restricting their access to the Israeli labor market in the 1990s.

While Israel today retains some of the characteristics of its more socialist-oriented economy of decades past, such as a national labor federation and universal health care, it long ago discarded the intensive state-run economic planning, strict currency and capital outflow controls, and high import duties that stifled international trade. The decisive turning point came in 1985, when Israel faced runaway hyperinflation that threatened to collapse the economy. Israel and the United States, led by Secretary of State George Schultz, jointly devised a stabilization program which entailed drastic currency devaluation, temporary price controls, decoupling wages from the inflation rate and sharp reductions in government spending and subsidies. These more "market-friendly" policies set the tone for further liberalization and privatization of the economy in later decades.

Today Israel's economy is firmly capitalist. Its macroeconomic indicators place it among the most advanced countries in the world. In 2014, the UN's Human Development Index ranked Israel 19th in the world, with a per capita gross national income, adjusted for purchasing power parity, of $30,000, placing it above countries such as France, Austria and Belgium. Its gross domestic product, also measured in purchasing power parity, stood at $268 billion, the 56th- largest economy in the world, ahead of similarly small-populated countries with advanced economies such as Denmark, Ireland and Finland.

Israel enjoys a reputation for having a high-tech, innovative, research-and-development-driven economy. Israel ranked second on Bloomberg's 2015 Global Innovation Index for research and development, trailing only South Korea. It ranked first in cyber security by the International Institute for Management Development in 2014. And it ranked third, behind only Switzerland and the United States, on the World Economic Forum's 2013–2014 capacity for innovation index. In 2013, the Startup Genome Project rated Tel Aviv, part of Israel's "Silicon Wadi" along its coastal plain, as the second-best start-up ecosystem globally, with more start-ups per capita than any place in the word and 61 companies listed on the NASDAQ.

**GLOSSARY**

## Purchasing power parity:
a measure to compare national incomes based on a real exchange rate derived from the cost of a common basket of goods.

In 2013, nearly 45 percent of Israel's industrial exports were in high-tech industries. Leading sectors comprising this high-tech export pie of $36 billion included computer services (24 percent), medical and computing equipment (22 percent), pharmaceutical products (18 percent) and electronic components (13 percent). Examples of these types of Israeli companies include Check Point Software Technologies, a global security provider for information technology, networks and data. Based in Tel Aviv, in 2014 Check Point had nearly 3,000 employees in four continents and was listed on the NASDAQ. Teva Pharmaceutical Industries, which traces its origins back to Palestine at the turn of the twentieth century, became the largest generic pharmaceutical company in the North American market in 2000. In 2012, it began trading on the New York Stock Exchange after moving over from the NASDAQ. Its subsidiary Teva Generics is the largest manufacturer of generic drugs in the world today.

**"The minute we fused intelligence capabilities with business capabilities, the Israeli high-tech economy just took off."**
**—Israeli Prime Minister Benjamin Netanyahu**

Two other industries play prominent roles in Israel's global economic profile: diamonds and weapons. In 2014, diamonds accounted for 15 percent of Israel's entire international trade, and from 2009 to 2013 diamonds were the single largest commodity exported by Israel. The Israel Diamond Exchange, located in Ramat Gan, near Tel Aviv, with more than 3,000 members and companies, is the largest diamond exchange in the world. Its roots date back to the pre-state British Mandate era. The preeminence Israel enjoys today in the global diamond market builds upon centuries of European Jewish expertise in the cutting and polishing of diamonds.

Even though Israel is the largest recipient of US military aid, it is a major player in the global weapons market in its own right. In 2014, Israel was the eighth-biggest exporter of weapons in the world, trailing only the five permanent members of the UN Security Council (the US, Russia, China, France and the UK), and Germany and Spain. Israel is the world's leader in the export of drones, a technology first developed in Israel beginning in the 1970s. Since 1985, Israeli-made drones have accounted for more than 60 percent of total drone sales worldwide; the United States comes in a distant second with a global market share of less than 25 percent. In 2013, three of the 100 largest weapons manufacturers were Israeli companies: Elbit Systems, Israel Aerospace Industries and Rafael together accounted for nearly $7.5 billion in arms sales that year.

Although Israel's high-tech and glitzy export economy generates significant wealth, as in the United States, its benefits do not trickle down equally to all segments of society. In fact, according to the Organization for Economic Cooperation and Development (OECD), Israel has the most unequal distribution of wealth in the developed world except for the United States. In Israel, the top ten percent earns 15 times more than the bottom ten percent (in the United States the ratio is 19:1 with the average for OECD countries at less than 10:1). This substantial income inequality and the high cost of living in Israel sparked massive protests in the summer of 2011. Tent cities sprung up in cities such as Tel Aviv as young Israelis lamented the lack of affordable housing. The movement culminated in a huge march of as many as 400,000 people (5 percent of the country's total population) in September 2011.

While the overall gap between haves and have-nots within Israeli society is striking, income inequality between Israeli Jews and Palestinian citizens of Israel is just as pronounced. According to a 2011 report by the Israel Democracy Institute, the wage gap between these groups expanded from 1997 to 2009, with Israeli Jews earning between 40 to 60 percent more than Palestinian citizens of Israel. This growing chasm is the product of both the Israeli government's under-resourcing of education and infrastructure in Palestinian communities within Israel and the pervasive societal discrimination faced by Palestinian citizens of Israel, both of which constrict their economic opportunities.

In coming years, the greatest challenge to be faced by the Israeli economy will not likely be its balance of payments, exchange rate, gross domestic product, or other traditional economic indicators. Instead this trial will be fundamentally political in nature. Since Israel implemented its military occupation of the Palestinian West Bank and Gaza Strip in 1967, its domination over Palestinian trade has created a captive market for Israeli exports, which accounted for nearly 60 percent of Palestinian imports in 2015. But as part of their growing discontent under Israeli occupation, Palestinians are actively boycotting Israeli products. In September 2015, the World Bank estimated that Palestinian imports of Israeli goods fell by nearly 25 percent in the first quarter of the year, attributable to "a growing trend among Palestinian consumers to substitute products imported from Israel by those from other countries."

This Palestinian consumer boycott of Israeli products is but one facet of a growing international movement to leverage economic pressure against Israel—and corporations which profit from its human rights abuses of Palestinians—to change the country's policies. In 2005, more than 170 Palestinian civil society groups launched a call for campaigns of boycott, divestment and sanctions (BDS), modeled on the campaign which helped generate international pressure on South Africa to end its apartheid system of government.

Since then, mainline churches such as the United Church of Christ and the Presbyterian Church (USA) have divested from US companies such as Caterpillar and Hewlett-Packard, which sell equipment to the Israeli military. Large multinational corporations such as Veolia have succumbed to pressure to sever their contracts providing services to Israeli settlements. And SodaStream, an Israeli

**FACTS**

In 2015, the Israeli government planned to allocate 100 million New Israeli Shekels (approximately $25 million) to fight BDS campaigns. In 2011, Israel's parliament passed a law enabling companies to sue Israelis who support BDS.

company, was forced to relocate its main manufacturing plant from an Israeli settlement in the West Bank. In June 2015, the Israeli government labeled the BDS movement a "strategic threat," but in the absence of progress toward a political resolution between Israel and the Palestinians, it is unlikely to be able to combat its growth.

## Sources:

Steve Forbes, "How The Small State Of Israel Is Becoming A High-Tech Superpower," Forbes, July 22, 2015, available at: https://www.forbes.com/sites/steveforbes/2015/07/22/how-the-small-state-of-israel-is-becoming-a-high-tech-superpower

"The World Factbook," Central Intelligence Agency, available at: https://www.cia.gov/library/publications/the-world-factbook/geos/is.html

"Statistical Abstract of Israel 2015," Central Bureau of Statistics, available at: http://www.cbs.gov.il/reader/shnaton/templ_shnaton_e.html?num_ab=st02_14&CYear=2015

"Table 1: Human Development Index and its components," UN Development Programme, available at: http://hdr.undp.org/en/content/table-1-human-development-index-and-its-components

"2nd Quarter 2015—Economic Highlights Presentation," Israeli Ministry of Finance, June 30, 2015, available at: http://www.financeisrael.mof.gov.il/FinanceIsrael/Pages/en/EconomicData/EconomicHighlights.aspx

Young Entrepreneur Council, "For Real Innovation, It's Not Silicon Valley But Silicon Wadi," Forbes, October 2, 2013, available at: http://www.forbes.com/sites/theyec/2013/10/02/for-real-innovation-its-not-silicon-valley-but-silicon-wadi/

"Israel Economy," The Israel Export and International Cooperation Institute, available at: http://www.export.gov.il/eng/Homepage/

"Our History," Teva Pharmaceutical Industries Ltd., available at: http://www.tevapharm.com/about/history/

"Doing Business in Israel—2014," BDO Ziv Haft, available at: http://www.bdo.co.il/_Uploads/dbsAttachedFiles/Doing_Business_in_Israel_2014.pdf

"Sectoral diversification in products for Israel's exports," International Trade Center, available at: http://www.intracen.org/layouts/CountryTemplate.aspx?pageid=47244645034&id=47244654313

"About the Diamond Exchange," Israel Diamond Exchange, available at: http://www.en.isde.co.il/article.aspx?id=23058

Stockholm International Peace Research Institute, available at: http://armstrade.sipri.org/armstrade/html/export_toplist.php

Rania Khalek, "Sixty percent of global drone exports come from Israel — new data," *Electronic Intifada*, March 24, 2015, available at: https://electronicintifada.net/blogs/rania-khalek/sixty-percent-global-drone-exports-come-israel-new-data

"The SIPRI Top 100 Arms-Producing Companies, 2013," Stockholm International Peace Research Institute, available at: http://www.sipri.org/research/armaments/production/recent-trends-in-arms-industry/The%20SIPRI%20Top%20100%202013.pdf

"OECD report: Inequality worst in Israel and US," *Times of Israel*, May 21, 2015, available at: http://www.timesofisrael.com/oecd-report-inequality-worst-in-israel-and-us

Isabel Kershner, "Summer of Protest in Israel Peaks With 400,000 in City Streets," *New York Times*, September 3, 2011, available at: http://www.nytimes.com/2011/09/04/world/middleeast/04israel.html?_r=0

Nadav Shemer, "Study: Income gap between Jews, Arabs grew in past decade," *Jerusalem Post*, November 24, 2011, available at: http://www.jpost.com/Business/Business-News/Study-Income-gap-between-Jews-Arabs-grew-in-past-decade

"Economic Monitoring Report to the Ad Hoc Liaison Committee," World Bank, September 30, 2015, available at: http://www-wds.worldbank.org/external/default/WDSContentServer/WDSP/IB/2015/09/29/090224b08310e894/2_0/Rendered/PDF/main0report.pdf

Britain's Lord Balfour inspects Rishon Le Zion, one of the original Zionist settlements, on a visit to Palestine in 1925.

# The Impending Clash: Zionism and Palestinians

Theodor Herzl was an unlikely figure to convene and preside over the First Zionist Congress in Basel, Switzerland in 1897, a conference which lay the foundations for the establishment of a Jewish state in Palestine one-half century later. Herzl was born into a secular Jewish family in Hungary. A commitment assimilationist, Herzl never learned Hebrew and would have been out of sorts in a traditional Jewish synagogue. As the Parisian correspondent for a Viennese newspaper, he was violently shaken from his worldview in 1895 by the rise of anti-Semitism in Austria and the trial of Alfred Dreyfus, a Jewish captain in the French Army who was falsely convicted of treason. The Dreyfus Affair surfaced latent anti-Semitism in French society, convincing Herzl that if even in France—the first European country to have granted Jewish people full civil rights—anti-Jewish bigotry could not be overcome, then assimilation as an answer to the "Jewish question" was not plausible. In an era of rising ethno-nationalism in Europe, Jews should establish their own state instead, Herzl concluded.

Herzl articulated his thoughts in an 1896 book entitled *The Jewish State*. As Herzl himself noted in the book, the idea of establishing a Jewish state was a "very old one" and that "no portion of my argument is based on a new discovery." Indeed the "return to Zion" had been a theme of Jewish spiritual longing since the Babylonian exile of the sixth century BCE and Herzl came somewhat belatedly to modern Zionism. Since the early 1880s, members of the Eastern

> The first modern, secular Zionist settlement in Palestine was named Rishon LeTzion—"The First to Zion"—and was founded by Ukrainian Jews in 1882. Located southeast of Tel Aviv, it is now the fourth-largest Israeli city.
>
> **FACTS**

European-based *Hovevei Zion* (Lovers of Zion) had been establishing Zionist settlements in Palestine, many of which received crucial financial backing from Baron Edmond Benjamin James de Rothschild, a committed Zionist. By the time Herzl published his book, more than one dozen Zionist settlements had already emerged.

Although Herzl cannot be credited with the invention of Zionism, it was his organizational drive, vision and leadership that galvanized the movement and created the institutions and political framework which would be necessary to turn this improbable vision into a reality. His slogan—"If you will it, it is no dream"—encapsulated the can-do attitude he brought to the movement's leadership. At the First Zionist Congress in Basel, Herzl was elected the head of the newly created international Zionist Organization, which still exists today as the World Zionist Organization. The congress adopted a political program which called for "the creation of a home for the Jewish people in Palestine to be secured by public law."

But what to do about the indigenous Palestinian population that already lived there? Early Zionist leaders adopted three distinct approaches to the question. The first attitude was to ignore the problem and not to grapple with its attendant moral issues, in effect pretending that Zionist colonization of Palestine did not involve the dispossession of its inhabitants. This view was neatly summarized in 1901 by the British Zionist Israel Zangwill, who contended that "Palestine is a country without a people; the Jews are a people without a country."

---

Palestinian opposition to Zionism emerged shortly after its inception. For example, the three-time mayor of Jerusalem, Yusuf Diya' al-Khalidi, wrote to Herzl in 1899 that although Zionism was "in theory a completely natural and just idea," Palestine's overwhelmingly Muslim and Christian population made it unjust. "By what right do the Jews demand it for themselves?" he asked. He warned that the Zionist project could not be accomplished peacefully, but could only come to fruition "by the force of cannons and warships."

The second approach acknowledged the existence of an indigenous people but believed that they should be removed from the land, either voluntarily through monetary inducements or compulsorily through the use of force, to make way for the Zionist project. Herzl preferred employing a light touch to this dispossession, confiding in his diary in 1895 that "when we occupy the land…we must expropriate gently the private property on the estates assigned to us. We shall try to spirit the penniless population across the border by procuring employment for it in the transit countries, while denying it any employment in our own country."

The third tack recognized the indigenous population and concluded that its dispossession was immoral. This view was taken by Ahad Ha'am, who after first visiting Palestine in 1891 wrote in "A Truth from *Eretz Yisrael* [The Land of Israel]: "We who live abroad are accustomed to believe that almost all *Eretz Yisrael* is now uninhabited desert and whoever wishes can buy land there as he pleases. But this is not true. It is very difficult to find in the land cultivated fields that are not used for planting." He upbraided Zionist settlers for their treatment of Palestinians. "They deal with the Arabs with hostility and cruelty, trespass unjustly, beat them shamefully for no sufficient reason, and even boast about their actions." Jettisoning the political goals of Zionism, Ha'am argued instead for a cultural form of Zionism which would not seek sovereignty.

During the first decades of Zionist colonization, the Ottoman Empire held ever-lessening sway over the Middle East as European colonial powers eagerly awaited the inevitable final

Although the Ottoman Empire was ruled by Muslims, its empire consisted of people from variegated religions and ethnicities. The Ottomans adopted what they referred to as a *millet* system, ensuring each community substantial religious autonomy and separate religious courts. This system prevailed in Palestine's Muslim, Christian and Jewish communities.

**FACTS**

carving up of the remaining territory of the "Sick Man of Europe," as it was known. In this period, Zionists purchased land, often from absentee landlords, displacing the farmers who tilled the soil as tenants. Palestinians plaintively petitioned the sultan in Istanbul to halt the dispossession, as in this 1890 letter from a Bedouin tribe that cultivated land in what became the Zionist settlement of Rehovot:

> "They began to expel us from the land we lived on… the farm, which was ours since the times of our fathers and grandfathers, was forcefully taken from us by the strangers who do not wish to treat us according to the accepted norms among tillers of the soil, and according to basic human norms or compassion. In short, they will not accept us, even as their slaves."

While succeeding in buying up tracts of land, the Zionist movement was not able to make substantial inroads in garnering official governmental support for its goal. Herzl painted Zionism as being beneficial to the interests of the Ottoman Empire. In the *Jewish State*, he publicly entreated Sultan Abdul Hamid II "to give us Palestine, we could in return undertake to regulate the whole finances of Turkey. We should there form a portion of a rampart of Europe against Asia, an outpost of civilization as opposed to barbarism." But the Ottoman Empire did not bite.

The decline of the Ottoman Empire and the rise of British Empire convinced Herzl that the fortunes of Zionism would best be served by hitching the movement to the empire on which the sun never set. In 1902 he wrote to the preeminent British colonialist Cecil Rhodes, attempting to recruit him to the cause. "You are being invited to help make history…it is something colonial and because it presupposes understanding of a development which will take twenty or thirty years…what I want you to do is not give me or lend me a few guineas, but to put the stamp of your authority on the Zionist plan and to make the following declaration to a few people who swear by you: I, Rhodes, have examined this plan and found it correct and practicable."

Unfortunately for Herzl, Rhodes died two months later, but his wooing of the British paid enormous dividends in 1917 when the British Foreign Secretary, Arthur James Balfour provided the political backing Zionism sought. The brief but consequential Balfour Declaration read: "His Majesty's Government view with favour the establishment in Palestine of a national home for the Jewish people, and will use their best endeavours to facilitate the achievement of this object, it being clearly understood that nothing shall be done which may prejudice the civil and religious rights of existing non-Jewish communities in Palestine, or the rights and political status enjoyed by Jews in any other country."

The declaration gained added significance after the British defeated the Ottomans during World War I and occupied Palestine. The League of Nations, the precursor of the United Nations, awarded Britain a "mandate" over Palestine in 1920. Under League of Nations mandates, the colonial powers were expected to prepare the population for self-determination and independence; however, the British Mandate in Palestine functioned differently from all others. By incorporating the Balfour Declaration into its mandate, Britain effectively pledged to work for the establishment of a Jewish homeland in Palestine even if the majority of the current population vehemently disagreed. "The weak point of our position," Balfour confessed to British Prime Minister David Lloyd George in 1919, "is of course that in the case of Palestine we deliberately and rightly decline to accept the principle of self-determination." The fundamentally anti-democratic nature of the British Mandate was

The commitment Great Britain made to the Zionist movement in the Balfour Declaration contradicted pledges it had previously made. In an exchange of letters from 1915 to 1916 between Hussein bin Ali, the Sharif of Mecca, and Sir Henry McMahon, the British High Commissioner in Egypt, Britain promised the Arab provinces of the Ottoman Empire to the sharif in exchange for rebelling against Ottoman rule.

encapsulated by Balfour's haughty letter to Lord George Curzon, his successor as Foreign Secretary:

"In Palestine we do not propose even to go through the form of consulting the wishes of the present inhabitants of the country… Zionism, be it right or wrong, good or bad, is rooted in age-long traditions, in present needs, in future hopes, of far profounder import than the desires and prejudices of the 700,000 Arabs who now inhabit that ancient land."

And with few exceptions over the next quarter-century, the British did just that: work with the leadership of the *yishuv*, the Jewish community in Palestine, to create the institutions necessary to establish a Jewish state. In 1930, the British recognized the Jewish Agency for Palestine, a quasi-government-in-waiting which handled both foreign relations for the *yishuv* and coordinated Jewish immigration to Palestine, both licitly and clandestinely beyond British quotas. The *yishuv* also formed a paramilitary organization, the Haganah ("Defense"), in 1920. Although the British never officially recognized

**Palestinians protest the Zionist movement outside the walls of the Old City of Jerusalem, March 1920**

David Ben-Gurion, born David Green in Poland in 1886, was the leading figure within the *yishuv*, Palestine's Jewish community, and became Israel's first prime minister after the country's founding in 1948. In 1920 he helped found the Histadrut, a Jewish-only labor union in Palestine and served as its General Secretary from 1921 to 1935. From 1935 to 1948, he chaired the executive committee of the Jewish Agency.

the Haganah, its presence was tolerated and the British collaborated with it especially during its brutal suppression of the Arab Revolt in Palestine from 1936 to 1939.

This three-year nationwide uprising against British colonial rule, a combination of urban strikes and other civil disobedience coordinated by the Arab Higher Committee and armed rural insurrection, played a seminal role in consolidating Palestinian national identity and in decelerating Britain's drive to turn Palestine over to the Zionist movement. Although the Peel Commission, appointed by the British government to investigate the causes of the Arab Revolt, did recommend in 1937 the partitioning of Palestine into two states—the first formal proposal to do so—the Arab Revolt also succeeded in pressuring the British into issuing a White Paper in 1939. This policy limited Jewish immigration to Palestine to 75,000 people over five years; additional immigration beyond that period would be subject to Palestinian acquiescence. It also foreclosed the possibility of partitioning Palestine and establishing a Jewish state; instead, the policy more nebulously called for the creation of a recognized "Jewish national home" in Palestine within the next decade. The White Paper was a complete debacle for the Zionist movement and appeared to have put the kibosh on its goals.

World War II, the Nazi extermination of an estimated six million European Jews in the Holocaust, the post-war retrenchment of an exhausted British Empire, and the rise of the United States as the new post-war superpower all played momentous roles in reversing the fortunes of the Zionist movement.

Anticipating the leading post-war role the United States would play in international affairs, President Franklin Delano Roosevelt sent Lt. Col. Harry Hoskins on a three-month tour of the Middle East in 1943 to recommend political options to him. Hoskins reported to the president that "Arab feelings remain uncompromisingly against the acceptance of a political Zionist State in Palestine." He warned that "only by military force can a Zionist State in Palestine be imposed upon the Arabs." Roosevelt dithered on formulating a policy toward Palestine; his death in 1945 thrust the issue into the lap of his successor, President Harry Truman.

Hitler's genocide against Jews generated tremendous guilt and reservoirs of sympathy for the aims of Zionism, especially in the United States and Europe. The misery of the Jewish survivors in displaced persons camps greatly affected Truman, who urged Britain to admit 100,000 Jews to Palestine on humanitarian grounds. Britain, however, having grown despondent over its ability to fix the mess it had created in Palestine, washed its hands of the issue and turned it over to the newly created United Nations. In 1947, a UN Special Committee on Palestine revived the idea of partitioning Palestine into two states: a Jewish State comprising 55 percent of Palestine and an Arab State comprising 45 percent. The General Assembly, under heavy US pressure, voted to adopt the recommendation. At the time of the partition recommendation, the Zionist movement owned just seven percent of Palestine and accounted for approximately one-third of its population. Indigenous Palestinians—Muslims and Christians—accounted for two-thirds of the population and resided on the vast majority of the land.

---

**FACTS**

In 1890, shortly after the advent of modern political Zionism, Palestine had an estimated total population of 532,000 people of whom 432,000 were Muslim, 57,000 Christian and 43,000 Jewish. At the time of the UN Partition Plan in 1947, the population had nearly quadrupled to 1,970,000, of whom 1,181,000 were Muslim, 630,000 Jewish and 143,000 Christian.

## SOURCES:

Theodor Herzl, *The Jewish State*, Project Gutenberg EBook, May 2, 2008, available at: https://www.gutenberg.org/files/25282/25282-h/25282-h.htm

Mark Tessler, *A History of the Israeli-Palestinian Conflict*, Indiana University Press, 1994, p. 48.

Adam Garfinkle, "On the Origin, Meaning, Use and Abuse of a Phrase," *Middle Eastern Studies*, Vol. 27, No. 4 (October 1991), p. 540, available at: http://blogs.brandeis.edu/siis/files/2014/04/garfinkle.pdf

Nur Masalha, *Expulsion of the Palestinians: The Concept of "Transfer" in Zionist Political Thought, 1882-1948*, Institute for Palestine Studies, Washington, DC, 1992, p. 9.

Ahad Ha'am, "A Truth from Eretz Yisrael," translated by Hilla Dayan, in *Wrestling with Zion: Progressive Jewish-American Responses to the Israeli-Palestinian Conflict*, Tony Kushner and Alisa Solomon (editors), Grove Press, 2003, pp. 14-16.

Nir Hasson, "New Documents Reveal Early Palestinian Attitudes Toward Zionist Settlement," *Haaretz*, November 4, 2012, available at: http://www.haaretz.com/israel-news/new-documents-reveal-early-palestinian-attitudes-toward-zionist-settlements-1.475085

Eitan Bar-Yosef, "A Village in the Jungle: Herzl, Zionist Culture, and the Great African Adventure," in *Theodor Herzl: From Europe to Zion*, Mark Gelber and Vivian Liska (editors), deGruyter, 2007, p. 101.

Anthony Nutting, "Balfour and Palestine: A Legacy of Deceit," Council for the Advancement of Arab-British Understanding, available at: http://www.balfourproject.org/balfour-and-palestine

"Summary of Lieutenant Colonel Harold B. Hoskins' Report on the Near East," Foreign Relations of the United States, 1943, Volume 4, US Department of State, pp. 782-784, available at: http://digicoll.library.wisc.edu/cgi-bin/FRUS/FRUS-idx?type=goto&id=FRUS.FRUS1943v04&isize=M&submit=Go+to+page&page=782

Rashid Khalidi, *Palestinian Identity: The Construction of Modern National Consciousness*, Columbia University Press, 1997, p. 75

The Old City of Jerusalem with the Dome of the Rock in the foreground, and parts of the modern city in the background.

# Jerusalem: Its Religious and Political Significance

If there was a formal designation for the place on earth with the most religious significance for the most believers, then the Old City of Jerusalem would win hands down. Densely packed within Ottoman Empire-era stone walls encompassing an area of less than one square kilometer are the sites at the epicenter of Jewish and Christian tradition and the holiest site outside of the Arabian Peninsula for Muslims. This proximity of religious sites attracts residents and devotees from all corners of the world, making Jerusalem a unique jumble of ethnicities, languages and cultures. On any given day, one can walk the narrow streets of the Old City and encounter Muslims from Indonesia studying the Quran on the Noble Sanctuary, Christians from Mexico retreading Jesus' final steps along the Via Dolorosa, or Jews from France celebrating a bar mitzvah at the Western Wall. But Jerusalem today is far from an interreligious idyll. Its religious significance for these three monotheistic faiths makes political control over Jerusalem one of the most hotly contested issues in contemporary international relations.

Jerusalem is one of the oldest cities in the world, with archaeological evidence indicating its habitation as much as four millennia

---

### Jerusalem:

In Hebrew, Jerusalem is *Yerushalayim*, often translated as "City of Peace." In Arabic, Jerusalem is *Al-Quds*, meaning "The Holy One."
In Arabic, the Islamic **holy sites of Jerusalem** are referred to as *Al-Haram Ash-Shareef*, "The Noble Sanctuary." In Hebrew, this site is called *Har Ha-Bayit*, translated as "Temple Mount."

**GLOSSARY**

before Jesus. Jerusalem holds religious significance in the Jewish tradition from as far back as the Book of Genesis, in which God commanded Abraham, regarded as the first Jew, to sacrifice his son Isaac on Mount Moriah, which Jewish tradition locates in today's Old City of Jerusalem. The city gained political significance in Judaism when David, proclaimed king of a short-lived unified Israelite monarchy, captured it from the Jebusites in approximately 1000 BCE and made it his capital. His son, King Solomon, built the First Temple there, making Jerusalem into a center of Jewish religious pilgrimage. This temple was destroyed by the Babylonian Empire in 586 BCE and the inhabitants of the Kingdom of Judea (long since split off from the then-defunct Kingdom of Israel) were exiled to Mesopotamia. Their fortunes were reversed, however, when the Persian Empire routed the Babylonians. In 539 BCE, King Cyrus allowed the Judeans to return and the Second Temple was built beginning in 520 BCE. The Second Temple stood for nearly six centuries, under the sovereignty of a variety of empires, until the Roman Empire destroyed it in 70 CE as part of its suppression of a Jewish revolt against its rule.

**DID YOU KNOW?**

Far from being a "City of Peace," Jerusalem has witnessed nearly incessant warfare over its six millennia of existence. According to Eric Cline, in *Jerusalem Besieged*, the city has been "destroyed at least twice, besieged 23 times, attacked an additional 52 times, and captured and recaptured 44 times."

Today religious Jews fervently pray for the restoration of the temple at the Western Wall, believed to be an outer retaining structure of the Second Temple, which was located above it on what Jews refer to as the Temple Mount. Traditionally Jewish people refrained from walking atop the Temple Mount, afraid that they would step on the location of the Holy of Holies, accessible only to the High Priest, and held that the rebuilding of the temple would be a divine act. However, Israel's military occupation of

East Jerusalem, in which the Old City is located, in 1967, sparked messianic urgings among some Jews and transmogrified the rebuilding of the temple into a temporal, political campaign. For example, during the war, the Israeli army's Chief Rabbi Shlomo Goren, urged the commanding general to "put 100 kg of dynamite into the Dome of the Rock [located on the Noble Sanctuary/ Temple Mount], and that will be it. Once and for all we will be rid of it." Fortunately, cooler heads prevailed and Muslim holy sites were not blown up by Israel, an act which could have sparked an all-out religious war. Today, however, various Jewish organizations promoting the rebuilding of the temple enjoy governmental funding and political support from Israeli ministers, turning a once fringe movement into a more mainstream undertaking.

Jerusalem is also sacred to Christians as the location of Jesus' final days, known as Passion Week, which commenced with Jesus riding into the city on a donkey, fulfilling a biblical prophecy announcing the arrival of the King of the Jews. According to most Gospels, Jesus then overturned the tables of the money changers in the temple, accusing them of venality, an act which heightened tensions with the Jewish religious establishment in the city. In short order thereafter, according to the Gospels, Jesus held his Last Supper with his disciples and predicted his betrayal, was arrested and tried by the Sanhedrin, a Jewish judicial body, and the Romans, and was crucified, buried and resurrected.

The Roman Emperor Constantine, who reigned from 306 to 337 CE, ceased the empire's persecutions of Christians and became the first emperor to convert to Christianity, thereby yoking what had been a small, despised religious community to the muscle of the world's superpower. Constantine's mother, Helena, a devout Christian, made a pilgrimage to Jerusalem in which she claimed to have discovered the cross upon which Jesus was crucified. It was here in approximately 325 CE that Constantine ordered the construction of the Church of the Holy Sepulchre, which Christians revere today as the site of Jesus' crucifixion, entombment and resurrection. Today six Christian denominations—the Greek Orthodox Church, the Franciscan Order of the Roman Catholic Church, the Armenian Apostolic Church, the Syrian Orthodox Church of Antioch, the Coptic Church, and the Ethiopian Orthodox Church—uneasily share the space with denominational feuds mediated by Muslim gatekeepers and holders of the church's keys, and sometimes by Israeli police as well.

Christian rule over Jerusalem continued under the Byzantine Empire until 637 CE when the city fell to the forces of Caliph Umar ibn al-Khattab, the second successor to lead the Muslim community following the death of the Prophet Muhammed, the founder of Islam, in 632 CE. The Muslim conquest of Jerusalem was part of Islam's lightening expansion out of the Arabian Peninsula, where Islam had begun, throughout the Middle East and North Africa in the seventh century. In 689 CE, under the orders of the Umayyad Caliph Abd al-Malik, the Dome of the Rock was built in Jerusalem. The golden-domed and intricately layered, mosaic-tiled structure houses the Foundation Stone, the place where Muslims believe that Abraham prepared to sacrifice his son Ismail according to God's command. Next to the Dome of the Rock is Al-Aqsa Mosque, which was built in the same time period. Meaning "the farthest mosque," it commemorates the spot from which Muslims believe that the Prophet Muhammed ascended to heaven to speak with God. It was also the original *qibla*, the direction in which Muslims turn to pray, before the Prophet Muhammed changed it to Mecca. Together Muslims refer to these two structures as the Noble Sanctuary and they are considered the third holiest site in Islam after Mecca and Medina.

A tenuous status quo has now taken hold over this site, holy both to Islam and Judaism. While Israel maintains control over the Noble Sanctuary/Temple Mount, and its police frequently raid it to quell Palestinian protests, under the terms of a 1994 peace treaty with Jordan, the latter country remains the custodian and administrator of the Islamic holy sites, a holdover function from the years it had annexed the Palestinian West Bank (1949–1967). Under this agreement, only Muslims are allowed to pray, but all are

> **FACTS**
>
> Israel's current Jerusalem Municipal Master Plan aims to ensure a 60:40 demographic split between Israelis Jews and Palestinians through 2020. Israel maintains this current Jewish majority in the city by building illegal settlements in East Jerusalem and by demolishing Palestinian homes and revoking Palestinians' residency status.

allowed to visit. Tensions erupt when groups of extremist Israeli Jews, who openly advocate for the destruction of the Islamic holy sites and the rebuilding of the Jewish temple, provocatively tour the area with large armed police forces accompanying them and sometimes attempt to pray.

With the exception of a brief interlude from 1099 to 1187, when the Crusaders ruled over Jerusalem, the city remained under the jurisdiction of various Islamic empires. This lasted until the Turkish Ottoman Empire was defeated in World War I and the British Empire assumed control over Jerusalem until 1948.

In recognition of Jerusalem's sacred status in Judaism, Christianity and Islam, the United Nations General Assembly recommended that the city and its environs be a *corpus separatum*, placed under international administration, not under the sovereignty of either the Jewish or Arab State envisioned in its proposed Partition Plan. This plan was vitiated, however, by warfare and the Israeli-Jordanian armistice agreement which divided the city in two, with Israel controlling West Jerusalem and Jordan governing East Jerusalem, including the Old City. In 1967, Israel conquered and annexed East Jerusalem, proclaiming the city to be its "eternal, undivided capital." The international community, however, does not recognize the validity of Israel's claims of sovereignty over Jerusalem, which is why almost all countries, including the United States, maintain their embassies to Israel in Tel Aviv. The United States views the status of Jerusalem as an issue which must be resolved in permanent-status talks between Israel and the Palestinians.

## SOURCES:

Thomas Idinopulos, *Jerusalem Blessed, Jerusalem Cursed: Jews, Christians, and Muslims in the Holy City from David's Time to Our Own*, Ivan R. Dee, Chicago, 1991, p. xi-xiv.

Yoel Cohen, "The Political Role of the Israeli Chief Rabbinate in the Temple Mount Question," *Jewish Political Studies Review*, Volume 11:1-2, Spring 1999, available at: http://www.jcpa.org/jpsr/s99-yc.htm

"Misperceptions Regarding Tensions Over the Noble Sanctuary," Institute for Middle East Understanding, September 15, 2015, available at: http://imeu.org/article/misperceptions-re-tensions-over-the-noble-sanctuary

"The Different Denominations in The Church of the Holy Sepulchre," November 10, 2011, Holy Crosses, available at: http://www.holycrossstore.com/interesting-reading/the-different-denominations-in-the-church-of-the-holy-sepulchre/

# HISTORY OF ISRAEL

**1948**
The State of Israel declares its independence after the UN recommends partitioning Palestine and Britain ends its mandate.

**1949**
David Ben-Gurion becomes the first elected prime minister of Israel after his Mapai party won 46 of 120 Knesset seats.

Israel signs armistice agreements with Egypt, Jordan, Syria and Lebanon, giving it sovereignty over 78 percent of historic Palestine.

**1967**
Israel conquers the Palestinian West Bank from Jordan and Gaza Strip from Egypt, instituting a military occupation that placed Israel in complete control of historic Palestine.

**1969**
Golda Meir becomes Israel's first female prime minister following Levi Eshkol's death in office; later that year, Labor wins an election with her at the party's helm, returning her to office.

**1977**
Menachem Begin of the Likud party becomes prime minister, breaking the nearly three-decade monopoly of power previously held by the Mapai/Labor party.

**1993**
Israel signs the Declaration of Principles with the Palestine Liberation Organization, ushering in two decades of an inconclusive "peace process."

**1995**
Yitzhak Rabin becomes the first Israeli prime minister to be assassinated, killed by a religious Jewish extremist who opposed the "peace process," following an appearance at a peace rally in Tel Aviv.

**2015**
Benjamin Netanyahu, of the Likud party, becomes prime minister for his fourth term, tying Ben-Gurion for the most terms served at the helm of the government.

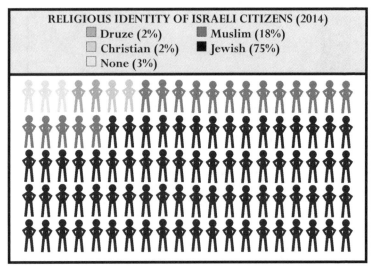

**RELIGIOUS IDENTITY OF ISRAELI CITIZENS (2014)**
Druze (2%)    Muslim (18%)
Christian (2%)    Jewish (75%)
None (3%)

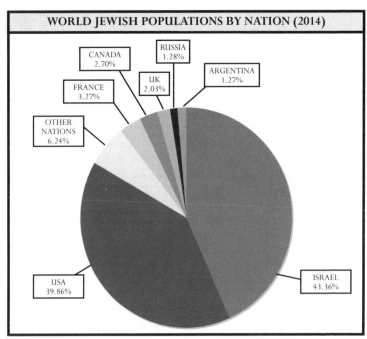

**WORLD JEWISH POPULATIONS BY NATION (2014)**

CANADA
2.70%

RUSSIA
1.28%

FRANCE
3.27%

UK
2.03%

ARGENTINA
1.27%

OTHER
NATIONS
6.24%

USA
39.86%

ISRAEL
43.36%

# Who Is Who?
# Israelis, Jews and Zionists

Israelis are citizens of the State of Israel. In 2014, 75 percent of Israel's population was Jewish. The remaining 25 percent of Israel's population was composed of Muslims (18 percent), Christians (2 percent) and Druze (2 percent)—an offshoot of Islam. The remaining 3 percent of the population was not categorized by religion.

Jews are individuals who identify religiously and/or culturally with Judaism. Jewish people can be of any ethnicity or nationality. In 2014, Israel had the world's largest Jewish population— 6.2 million, of an estimated global population of 14.3 million. The next-largest Jewish communities were in the United States (5.7 million), France (467,000), Canada (386,000), United Kingdom (290,000), Russian Federation (183,000) and Argentina (181,000).

Zionists are adherents of a political program to create and maintain a Jewish State in part, or all of, historic Palestine. Almost all Israeli Jews define themselves as Zionist, although a small minority rejects Zionism. Palestinian citizens of Israel are not Zionists, viewing it as discriminatory. In the United States, most major Jewish American organizations are Zionist; however, some Jewish Americans are Zionists while others are

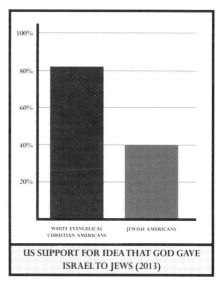

WHITE EVANGELICAL CHRISTIAN AMERICANS    JEWISH AMERICANS

**US SUPPORT FOR IDEA THAT GOD GAVE ISRAEL TO JEWS (2013)**

not. The Pew Research Center found in 2013 that 82 percent of white Christian evangelicals supported the notion that God gave Israel to the Jewish people; 40 percent of Jewish Americans agreed.

## SOURCES:

Statistical Abstract of Israel—2015, available at: http://www.cbs.gov.il/reader/shnaton/templ_shnaton_e.html?num_tab=st02_02&CYear=2015 and http://www.cbs.gov.il/reader/shnaton/templ_shnaton_e.html?num_tab=st02_02&CYear=2015

Michael Lipka, "More white evangelicals than American Jews say God gave Israel to the Jewish people," Pew Research Center, October 3, 2013, available at: http://www.pewresearch.org/fact-tank/2013/10/03/more-white-evangelicals-than-american-jews-say-god-gave-israel-to-the-jewish-people/

# Israel Establishes Hegemony over Palestine

The Jewish community in Palestine, known as the *yishuv*, greeted the UN Partition Plan euphorically. In its eyes, the vote bestowed an international imprimatur on Zionism's quest to establish a Jewish state. Palestinians, meanwhile, reacted with a mixture of outrage and trepidation. How could a newly created international body divide Palestine against the wishes of the majority of its inhabitants?

While the Palestinian leadership rejected the plan outright as an unjust imposition which violated the principles of self-determination, the Zionist movement adopted a more nuanced position, welcoming the plan in principle but not committing to its proposed borders.

Even if the two sides had agreed to peacefully partition the land, the demographics on the ground rendered the idea moot. With the Zionist movement owning just seven percent of the land and the Jewish population largely clustered in small, urban areas and scattered farming communities, there was no way to create a viable Jewish state without the massive displacement of the indigenous Palestinian population. The UN's plan reflected this predicament: the Jewish state it advocated for establishing in 55 percent of Palestine was actually a binational state, with a slim majority of Jewish inhabitants (538,000 versus 397,000 Palestinians).

During the twilight, chaotic days of the British Mandate, the Zionist leadership adopted a plan of action that would dramatically alter this demographic balance. In March 1948, Zionist political and military leaders approved Plan D, a military campaign to drive out as many Palestinians from as much of Palestine as possible, both before and after the British departure. "The plan," according to Israeli historian Ilan Pappe, author of *The Ethnic Cleansing of Palestine*, "and above all its systematic implementation in the following months, was a clear-cut case of an ethnic cleansing operation, regarded under international law today as a crime against humanity."

Months before neighboring Arab countries went to war with the newly established State of Israel in May 1948, Zionist militias began this ethnic cleansing campaign under the watchful eyes of the departing British, forcibly expelling approximately 250,000 Palestinians. Palestinians also fled in terror from advancing Zionist militias, especially after the massacre and mutilation of more than 100 Palestinian civilians killed by the Irgun militia in Deir Yassin, a village near Jerusalem, in April 1948, one of dozens of such atrocities committed first by Zionist militias and later by the Israeli military after the state's establishment.

Israel signed armistice agreements with Jordan, Egypt, Syria and Lebanon in 1949, which left Israel in control of 78 percent of historic Palestine. Palestinian independence on the remaining 22 percent of their land was precluded by a prearranged understanding between Israel and Jordan that the latter would annex what became known as the West Bank; Egypt placed the Gaza Strip under military rule.

**Palestinians driven into Jaffa Harbor, April 1948**

Israel had achieved massive success in its premeditated ethnic cleansing campaign: at least 750,000 Palestinians became refugees. More than 80 percent of Palestinians who had previously lived in what became Israel were forcibly expelled or had fled for their lives. Israel razed 531 Palestinian villages and emptied 11 Palestinian urban neighborhoods of their residents in an attempt to erase all vestiges of Palestinian presence in the Jewish state. Israelis celebrate this era as their War of Independence; Palestinians mourn their dispossession as the *Nakba*, or catastrophe.

After the armistice agreements, Israel sought to consolidate this new demographic reality and imprint upon the state a Jewish character in two primary ways: by prohibiting Palestinian refugees from returning to their villages and cities, and by creating a two-tiered legal system which privileged Jewish citizens of the state and disadvantaged those Palestinians who remained.

International law grants refugees an unconditional right to return to their homes. In December 1948, the UN adopted the Universal Declaration of Human Rights, which states, "Everyone has the right

**Nahr al-Barid refugee camp**

to leave any country, including his own, and to return to his country." That same month, the UN recognized that this principle must pertain to Israel as well. It adopted General Assembly Resolution 194, declaring that Palestinian "refugees wishing to return to their homes and live at peace with their neighbours should be permitted to do so at the earliest practicable date." However, Israel has refused to allow Palestinian refugees to exercise their right of return, arguing that to do so would constitute a "demographic threat." As a result, Palestinians exiled from their homeland and their descendants continue to languish in refugee camps administered by the UN Relief and Works Agency for Palestine Refugees in the Near East. With more than five million registered refugees, the Palestine refugee crisis is both the longest-lasting and numerically largest one in the world.

In its first five years, Israel expropriated vast tracts of individual and communal Palestinian land, transferred its management to the state and subcontracted the planning for most state land to the Jewish National Fund, a nongovernmental organization whose charter reserves land for the exclusive use of Jewish people. The three laws through which this expropriation and land transfer took place—Absentees' Property Law (1950), Land Acquisition Law (1953) and Jewish National Fund Law (1953)—are still operative today and constitute a few of the more than 50 laws which discriminate against Palestinians in Israel.

Israel subjected those Palestinians who resisted its ethnic cleansing campaign and remained on their land to a harsh military rule which lasted until 1966. For example, Palestinians were forbidden to leave their villages without the authorization of an Israeli military governor. Many Palestinians within Israel remain internally displaced persons, disallowed from returning to their original lands just as Palestinian refugees are as well. In 2015, more than 20 percent of Israeli citizens were Palestinian. Although Palestinian citizens of Israel can vote and stand for office (the third-largest bloc in Israel's parliament today is a coalition of primarily Palestinian political parties), they continue to face legal and societal discrimination which adversely affects nearly every facet of life, from the unequal distribution of governmental allocations to prejudicial housing and land use rights to widespread racist attitudes among Jewish Israelis, rendering Palestinians within Israel second-class citizens.

In June 1967, Israel preemptively launched a war against Egypt after President Gamal Abdel Nasser ordered out of the Sinai Peninsula UN peacekeeping forces separating the two armies. The brief ensuing war dramatically redrew the boundaries of the Middle East: Israel occupied the remaining 22 percent of historic Palestine—the West Bank, including East Jerusalem and the Gaza Strip—in addition to the Egyptian Sinai Peninsula and Syrian Golan Heights (Israel withdrew from the Sinai Peninsula as part of a peace treaty with Egypt signed in 1979. Israel's refusal to return all of the Golan Heights to Syria and withdraw to its original armistice lines is the primary reason why intermittent Israeli-Syrian peace negotiations have not succeeded.)

The UN adopted Security Council Resolution 242 in November 1967. Citing the UN Charter's principle of the "inadmissibility of the acquisition of territory by war," the UN called for the "withdrawal of Israel armed forces from territories occupied in the recent conflict." In addition, the resolution called for the "termination of all claims or states of belligerency and respect for and acknowledgment of the sovereignty, territorial integrity and political independence of every State in the area and their right to live in peace within secure and recognized boundaries free from threats or acts of force." This resolution, known informally as the "land for peace" formula, has formed the basis for every subsequent Arab-Israeli peace initiative.

Israel, however, had other designs for the territory it now occupied. Its crushing victory unleashed jubilant, even messianic, fervor within segments of Israeli society. Especially in the Palestinian West Bank, Israeli Jews now visited—and sought dominion over—lands with historical and religious resonance. With Israel in control of the totality of historic Palestine, many Israeli Jews now felt that Zionism had reached its apotheosis. As a state embodying the ethos of a self-identified colonizing movement, it was, in a sense, predictable and logical that Israel would now continue its colonization of Palestinian land, heedless of the ramifications or condemnation of the international community.

Israel's colonization of Palestinian land in the West Bank and Gaza Strip began in earnest almost immediately, despite Israeli Prime Minister Levi Eshkol's awareness that doing so was flagrantly illegal. The Fourth Geneva Convention, which regulates the conduct of armies during belligerent military occupation, makes it illegal for the Occupying Power to "transfer parts of its own civilian population into the territory it occupies." The Israeli Foreign Ministry's own legal counsel even warned the government that this prohibition is "categorical and is not conditioned on the motives or purposes of the transfer, and is aimed at preventing colonization of conquered territory by citizens of the conquering state." But this admonishment fell on deaf ears. Today Israel maintains 170 Jewish-only settlements on Palestinian land in the West Bank and East Jerusalem, populated by 650,000 colonists. (Israel also colonized the Gaza Strip until 2005, when it unilaterally withdrew its settlements from this seaside enclave.)

Israel's colonization and expropriation of land is only one facet of a harsh and brutal regime of military occupation to which Palestinians in the West Bank and Gaza Strip have been subjected for the past half-century. Military Order 101, promulgated by the Israeli military in August 1967 and still in effect today, deprives Palestinians of civil and political rights. According to the Palestinian human rights group Addameer, it criminalizes organizing and participating in protests, waving flags or other political symbols, and distributing printed political material. Any political assembly of ten or more people is illegal without the permission of an Israeli military commander. Epitomizing the stringent repression and draconian control over Palestinian life is Israel's jailing of more than 800,000 Palestinians—or 40 percent of the male population—since 1967, sometimes without charge or trial, through "administrative detention." Israel also often routinely arrests, tortures and imprisons Palestinian children through its military judicial system, the only country in the world to try children in military courts.

While Israel subjects Palestinians to martial law, Israeli settlers enjoy the benefits of Israeli civil law, tax benefits from the state for colonizing Palestinian land, and infrastructure built exclusively for their use. This duality led Human Rights Watch to conclude "that Israel operates a two-tier system" whose policies "harshly discriminate against Palestinian residents, depriving them of basic necessities while providing lavish amenities for Jewish settlements."

After living under this regime of military occupation and colonization for a generation, Palestinians could abide it no longer. In December 1987, an Israeli driver killed several Palestinians in a traffic accident in Gaza, providing the fuse which sparked an intifada, or uprising. This largely nonviolent uprising was characterized by protests, tax resistance (Palestinians, in essence, were forced to pay for Israel's occupation through taxes) and boycotts of Israeli goods. These nonviolent, time-honored tactics garnered significant international sympathy for the Palestinian cause, especially as Israel responded ferociously, with Israeli Defense Minister Yitzhak Rabin ordering soldiers to break the bones of protesters.

The Palestine Liberation Organization—a coalition of Palestinian political groups founded in 1964, widely recognized as the "sole, legitimate representative of the Palestinian people" and chaired by Yasser Arafat—was slow to recognize the significance of the intifada from its backwater exile in Tunisia. The dynamics of the intifada were shifting the center of Palestinian political gravity away from this exile-led liberation movement toward the grassroots, on-the-ground leadership of this protest movement. The PLO's National Charter called for the establishment of one secular, democratic state in historic Palestine, with Jews, Christians and Muslims living as equals. But in November 1988, the PLO shifted its political program by adopting a declaration of independence, which called for a Palestinian state to be established in territories occupied by Israel in 1967.

Would the PLO's embrace of the two-state solution—a Palestinian state in the West Bank and Gaza Strip alongside Israel—offer a way out of the seemingly intractable morass? Perhaps so. Five years later, back-channel secret negotiations between Israel and the PLO, hosted by Norway, appeared to yield a stunning breakthrough.

## SOURCES:

Ilan Pappe, *The Ethnic Cleansing of Palestine*, Oneworld Publications, 2006.

Avi Shlaim, *Collusion Across the Jordan: King Abdullah, the Zionist Movement, and the Partition of Palestine*, Columbia University Press, 1998.

Universal Declaration of Human Rights, available at: http://www.un.org/en/documents/udhr/

United Nations General Assembly Resolution 194, available at: http://unispal.un.org/UNISPAL.NSF/0/C758572B78D1CD0085256BCF0077E51A

Adalah: The Legal Center for Arab Minority Rights in Israel, "Discriminatory Laws in Israel," available at: http://www.adalah.org/en/content/view/7771

United Nations Security Council Resolution 242, available at: http://unispal.un.org/UNISPAL.NSF/0/7D35E1F729DF491C85256EE700686136

Gershon Goremberg, *The Accidental Empire: Israel and the Birth of the Settlements, 1967-1977*, Macmillan, 2007.

"Israeli military orders relevant to the arrest, detention and prosecution of Palestinians," and "General Briefing: Palestinian Political Prisoners in Israeli Prisons Addameer: Prisoner Support and Human Rights Association," available at: http://www.addameer.org/israeli_military_judicial_system/military_orders and http://www.addameer.org/advocacy/briefings_papers/general-briefing-palestinian-political-prisoners-israeli-prisons

"Separate and Unequal: Israel's Discriminatory Treatment of Palestinians in the Occupied Palestinian Territories," Human Rights Watch, available at: https://www.hrw.org/news/2010/12/19/israel/west-bank-separate-and-unequal

## DO THE MATH

**1,951:** The number of Palestinian children who did not take part in hostilities and were killed by the Israeli military from September 2000 to September 2014.

**800,000:** The number of Palestinian olive trees uprooted by the Israeli military and settlers since 1967, the equivalent of razing every tree in New York's Central Park 33 times over.

**48,488:** The number of Palestinian homes and other structures destroyed by the Israeli military from 1967 to October 2015.

**0.7:** The percentage of state land in the Palestinian West Bank allocated for Palestinian use by Israel from 1980 to 2013.

**38:** The percentage of state land in the Palestinian West Bank allocated for Israeli settlements by Israel from 1980 to 2013.

**40:** The percentage of Palestinian males living under Israeli military occupation who have been jailed.

**99.74:** The percentage of Palestinians convicted of a charge before Israeli military courts.

**2.2:** The percentage of Israeli soldiers indicted after investigations into abuses against Palestinians and their property from 2010 to 2013.

## SOURCES:

"Distribution of Palestinian Child Fatalities by Month," Defense for Children International Palestine, available at: http://www.dci-palestine.org/child_fatalities_by_month

Visualizing Palestine, "Since 1967 Israel has razed over 800,000 Palestinian olive trees, the equivalent to destroying Central Park 33 times over," *Mondoweiss*, October 10, 2013, available at: http://mondoweiss.net/2013/10/palestinian-equivalent-destroying

"Did You Know That?" Israeli Committee Against House Demolitions, available at: http://www.ichad.org

Chaim Levenson, "Just 0.7% of State Land in the West Bank Has Been Allocated to Palestinians, Israel Admits," *Haaretz*, March 28, 2013, available at: http://www.haaretz.com/israel-news/just-0-7-of-state-land-in-the-west-bank-has-been-allocated-to-palestinians-israel-admits. premium-1.512126

"Isolation and Solitary Confinement of Palestinian Prisoners and Detainees in Israeli Facilities," Addameer: Prisoner Support and Human Rights Association, August 1, 2009, available at: http://www.addameer.org/publications/isolation-and-solitary-confinement-palestinian-prisoners-and-detainees-israeli

Noam Sheizaf, "Conviction rate for Palestinians in Israel's military courts: 99.74%," *+972 Magazine*, November 29, 2011, available at: http://972mag.com/conviction-rate-for-palestinians-in-israels-military-courts-99-74-percent/28579/

"Israeli human rights organizations B'Tselem and Yesh Din: Israel is unwilling to investigate harm caused to Palestinians," B'Tselem: The Israeli Information Center for Human Rights in the Occupied Territories, September 4, 2014, available at: http://www.btselem.org/press_releases/20140905_failure_to_investigate

## Israel's Diverse and Fractious Society

Throughout its history, all of Israel's prime ministers have hailed from European-Jewish backgrounds, presenting a distorted picture of Israel's ethnic diversity today to the outside world. The ethnic homogeneity of Israel's prime minister belies the fact that Israel is a majority non-white society.

In 2014, Israel's population stood at 8.2 million people. Of that total, 32 percent were at least second-generation Israeli-born Jewish people whose continent of origin is unknown, some of whom are children of parents from different continents. Twenty-four percent of Israel's population were either first-generation Israeli-born or born abroad from Jewish-European and -American backgrounds. Twenty-one percent of Israel's population was indigenous Palestinian; 19 percent of Israel's population were either first-generation Israeli-born or born abroad from Jewish-Asian and -African backgrounds. And 4 percent of the population is categorized by Israel as neither Jewish nor Palestinian.

Although Israel today is a diverse society, the early decades of Zionist colonization of Palestine were predominated by Jewish

> The four percent of Israel's population categorized as neither Jewish nor Palestinian include Circassians, a Muslim Caucasian people expelled from their ancestral homeland by Czarist Russia; Christian Armenians who immigrated to Jerusalem for religious purposes or survived the Ottoman Empire's genocidal campaign during World War I; and Hebrew Israelites, people of color, mostly African-Americans, who hold that they are the original Israelites but who are not recognized as being Jewish by the state.

**FACTS**

Europeans. Jewish immigration to Palestine (and later Israel)—known in Hebrew as *aliyah*, which literally means "ascension" but also has a religious connotation of making a pilgrimage to Jerusalem—came in waves. The First Aliyah, from 1882 to 1903, consisted of 25,000 Russian and Romanian Jews and 2,500 Yemeni Jews. The Second Aliyah, from 1904 to 1914, consisted of 35,000 primarily Russian and Polish Jews. The Third Aliyah, from 1919 to 1923, also consisted of 35,000 people, mainly from Russia and Poland with smaller numbers from Lithuania and Romania. The Fourth Aliyah, from 1924 to 1928, was the largest to date, consisting of 67,000 people primarily from the same countries as the previous wave of immigration, with smaller groups of Yemeni and Iraqi Jews. The Fifth Aliyah, from 1929 to 1939, the last and largest of the pre-state waves of immigration, consisted of more than 250,000 Jewish people from all corners of Europe. These pre-World War II immigrants came to Palestine for a variety of reasons: to fulfill their Zionist ideology, to escape anti-Jewish pogroms in Russia and to flee the ravages of World War I and the rising tide of Nazism.

With pre-World War II Zionist immigration to Palestine consisting almost exclusively of Jewish-Europeans, it was natural that this community would form the social, economic and political elite of the *yishuv*—the pre-state Jewish community in Palestine—and later on of Israel. It was not until after the founding of Israel that large-scale immigration of Jewish communities from the Arab world and non-Arab Middle Eastern countries, such as Iran, began. In 1949, Israel airlifted 50,000 Yemeni Jews, whose ancient community dated back

**DID YOU KNOW?**

Public transportation is shut down in Israel for the Jewish Sabbath, running from Friday night to Saturday night. All governmental services are closed as well, except in times of emergency. In some neighborhoods of Jerusalem, tensions run high between religious and secular Jews. Private cars may be stoned by ultra-Orthodox Jews who view automobile travel on the Sabbath as a sacrilege.

to biblical times. Between 1950 and 1951, more than 90 percent of Iraq's Jewish community of 135,000 people immigrated to Israel after intensive anti-Jewish and anti-Zionist governmental and societal backlash following Israel's establishment. The Iraqi government allowed members of the Jewish community to leave for Israel only after renouncing their Iraqi citizenship and forfeiting their property. One-quarter million Moroccan Jews—the largest community from an Arabic-speaking country—immigrated to Israel mostly between 1954 and 1964. Zionist agents in Morocco stoked fears among the Jewish community that their place in Moroccan society would become untenable after the country's independence from France in 1956. These suspicions proved largely unfounded; King Mohammed V had saved many Moroccan Jews from the Holocaust by refusing to implement the Vichy regime's anti-Jewish measures and encouraged Jewish people to remain in the kingdom after independence. Smaller Jewish communities from other North African countries, such as Egypt, Libya, Tunisia and Algeria, immigrated to Israel during this period as well.

In total, more than 850,000 Jewish people from Arab and other non-Arab Middle Eastern countries immigrated to Israel after its establishment in 1948, more than doubling its Jewish population. The Israeli government frequently argues that Israel's absorption of these Jewish communities should constitute an even population exchange with the approximately 750,000 Palestinians who fled or were expelled by Israel during its founding and that respective property claims should cancel each other out. This stance angers both Palestinian refugees and these Jewish communities because, as they rightfully point out, refugee and property rights belong to individuals, not collectives or nations.

The absorption of people from these Jewish communities—known as *Mizrahim* ("Easterners") or *Sephardim* (literally "Spaniards," but referring to the liturgy and rites of non-European Jews)—into Israel's dominant Ashkenazi (an ancient reference to Germany, but connoting the liturgy and rites of European Jews) society was not at all smooth. The sudden, massive influx of *Mizrahim* greatly strained the resources of the new state. Most *Mizrahim* were shunted off to *ma'abarot*, transit camps, which were often no more than tent cities. From these temporary encampments, most *Mizrahim* were resettled in development towns on Israel's periphery where few educational and economic opportunities existed.

In general, Ashkenazim tended to look down their noses at the different languages, cultures and rites their coreligionists brought to Israel. As in the United States during this period, the notion of a societal "melting pot" frequently meant that those differing from idealized "white" norms were encouraged, or even coerced, into blending in with the dominant culture. This paradigm was challenged beginning in the early 1970s by the Israeli Black Panthers (a nod to the African-American movement), who protested societal and governmental discrimination and articulated cultural self-assertion. This movement paved the way for a *Mizrahi* cultural renaissance and greater political power. The Shas party, founded in 1984, is today a major political player representing the concerns of *Mizrahi* communities. While today Israeli society, like US society, more closely resembles the "tossed salad" metaphor for multiculturalism, *Mizrahim* remain underrepresented in academia, media, industry and politics and overrepresented in Israel's jails.

Two other latter-day waves of immigration further transformed the face of Israeli society. Shortly before and following the collapse of the Soviet Union in 1991, an estimated one million people immigrated to Israel. Slightly more than half of these immigrants were not Jewish, but qualified for Israeli citizenship due to their familial relationship with Jews from the former Soviet Union. This substantial arrival of so many people in such a short time span (one in six non-Palestinian Israeli citizens now speaks Russian as his or her first language) quickly made a separate Russian-Israeli culture bloom. For example, by 2004, there were four Russian language daily newspapers in Israel, eleven weeklies, five monthlies and more than 50 local papers, according to Zvi Gitelman.

In 1984 and 1991, Israel airlifted 22,000 Ethiopian Jews, joining 8,000 compatriots who began immigrating to Israel in the late 1970s. In 2014, the Ethiopian Jewish population of Israel was approximately 130,000 people, or two percent of Israel's total Jewish population. Israel often touts its absorption of the Ethiopian Jewish community as evidence of its nonracist character. However, Ethiopian Jews have faced discrimination in Israel. Incidents of Israeli health officials forcibly giving Ethiopian Jewish women injections of long-term birth control, the refusal of Israel's version of the Red Cross to accept donations of blood from Ethiopian Jews, and cases of police brutality have periodically roiled the community.

Israel currently has nearly 50,000 African asylum seekers. Most are from Eritrea (73 percent) and Sudan (19 percent), according to the African Refugee Development Center in Israel. Life is harsh for asylum seekers in Israel. They are denied the right to legally work. Asylum seekers in Tel Aviv have been attacked by Israeli Jewish mobs, and Israel detains many asylum seekers in a desert prison camp.

**FACTS**

While these ethnic divisions within Israeli Jewish society create real vicissitudes, they pale in comparison to the fundamental and perhaps unbridgeable chasm between Israeli Jews and Palestinian citizens of Israel. The Palestinian survivors—and their descendents—Israel's original ethnic cleansing campaign of 1948 now account for more than one in five Israeli citizens and speak Arabic, rather than Hebrew, as their first language. Israel's insistence on being defined as a "Jewish state" points to an inherent contradiction between its claims to democracy and the exclusivist nature of a country with laws and societal mores that privilege Jewish identity and discriminate against its indigenous citizens.

Israel points to individual Palestinian citizens of Israel such as Salim Joubran, who sits on Israel's Supreme Court, as evidence that it is a color-blind meritocracy. But just as Thurgood Marshall's appointment to the Supreme Court did not mean that racism and discrimination against African-Americans had been eradicated, so

**DID YOU KNOW?**

There is no civil marriage in Israel. Instead, all citizens of Israel must be married in a religious ceremony. Marriages between Israelis of different faiths, while infrequent, cannot be performed in the country. Instead couples in mixed marriages or those who prefer a secular wedding ceremony must be wed abroad. Cyprus is a close, popular destination for Israelis wanting a civil marriage ceremony.

too do Palestinian citizens of Israel continue to suffer from pervasive and systemic racism and discrimination which makes them at best second-class citizens and at worst viewed as a "fifth column" by Israeli Jews. For example, Israel retains an almost exclusively separate-and-unequal public school system strictly segregated by language and systemically underfunded in Palestinian communities. According to Adalah: The Legal Center for Arab Minority Rights in Israel, there are more than 50 Israeli laws which discriminate against Palestinian citizens of Israel, negatively affecting every aspect of their life from land use and planning to governmental benefits to residency and marriage rights (a Palestinian citizen of Israel is not allowed to live in Israel with a Palestinian spouse from the West Bank or Gaza Strip).

## Sources:

"Statistical Abstract of Israel 2015," available at:
http://www.cbs.gov.il/reader/shnaton/templ_shnaton_e.html?num_tab=st02_08x&CYear=2015 and http://www.cbs.gov.il/reader/shnaton/templ_shnaton_e.html?num_tab=st02_01&CYear=2015

"About Israel," Ministry of Aliyah and Immigrant Absorption, http://www.moia.gov.il/English/FeelingIsrael/AboutIsrael/Pages/default.aspx

Warren Hoge, "Group seeks justice for 'forgotten' Jews," *New York Times*, November 5, 2007, available at:
http://www.nytimes.com/2007/11/04/world/americas/04iht-nations.4.8182206.html?_r=0

Zvi Gitelman, "The 'Russian Revolution' in Israel," in Alan Dowty, *Critical Issues in Israeli Society*, Greenwood Publishing Group, 2004, p. 99.

# Perpetual Emergency

Israel is in a state of perpetual emergency—not figuratively, in the sense of feeling continuously insecure, but literally. Upon its establishment in 1948, Israel incorporated into its laws the Defense (Emergency) Regulations originally issued by the British Mandate-era government in 1945. These were a compilation of more than 100 emergency regulations issued by the British beginning in the 1930s to suppress the Arab Revolt and illicit Zionist militias.

Unless otherwise annulled by the Knesset—Israel's parliament—these regulations remain in effect today and grant the government sweeping powers which infringe upon civil and human rights. These regulations, for example, allow the government to hold someone indefinitely without charge or trial (a procedure known as "administrative detention"), demolish houses as a punitive measure and expel people from the country.

These draconian emergency regulations formed the basis for the martial law Israel imposed on Palestinian citizens of the state until 1966. Although these regulations are infrequently used in Israel itself today, they remain the bedrock of the judicial system for Israel's military occupation of the Palestinian West Bank and Gaza Strip.

Aside from this perpetual state of emergency, a few other attributes of the state make it appear inchoate. For example, Israel lacks a constitution. Instead, the Knesset has passed a series of Basic Laws which enshrine citizens' rights. However, these laws can be amended or overturned by parliament. In addition, Basic Laws can also serve to discriminate against non-Jews living under Israel's rule. For example, the 1980 Jerusalem Law codifies Israel's illegal annexation of Palestinian East Jerusalem, maintaining a separate and unequal system in which Palestinian Jerusalemites only have resident status, rather than citizenship.

In addition, while Israel has permanent borders with Egypt and Jordan, formalized by peace treaties, it has only temporary armistice lines with Syria and Lebanon, signed in 1949. And Israel's illegal colonization of the Palestinian West Bank has eviscerated its former armistice line with Jordan, known as the Green Line.

## SOURCES:

"Defense (Emergency) Regulations," *B'Tselem* - The Israeli Information Center for Human Rights in the Occupied Territories, available at: http://www.btselem.org/legal_documents/emergency_regulations

# The Peace Process and Its Demise

After the US-led coalition's drubbing of Iraq in the 1990–1991 Gulf War, President George H. W. Bush sought to birth a "new world order." Part of his vision included resolving the Arab–Israeli conflict in general and the Israeli-Palestinian issue in particular. Toward this end, the US and the Soviet Union convened the Madrid Peace Conference in October and November 1991. At the time, Israel was still refusing to speak with its nemesis, the PLO. Nominally, a joint Jordanian-Palestinian delegation independent of the PLO negotiated on behalf of Palestinians; in reality, the delegation adjourned for frequent consultations with the PLO's leadership in Tunisia.

Although the subsequent negotiating sessions petered out without any major breakthroughs, they did make clear that direct negotiations between Israel and the PLO were inevitable if the Israeli-Palestinian issue were ever to be resolved. Israelis elected a more left-leaning government in June 1992, headed by Prime Minister Yitzhak Rabin, who temporarily froze the expansion of Israeli settlements in occupied Palestinian land and authorized direct contact with the PLO.

Informal discussions in Oslo, shepherded by the Norwegian government, led to formal contacts and eventually a once unimaginable advance: a Declaration of Principles between Israel and the PLO setting out a five-year incremental process to resolve all outstanding issues. Yasser Arafat sent Rabin a letter recognizing the State of Israel, thereby ceding Palestinian territorial claims over 78 percent of historic Palestine; in exchange, Rabin merely recognized the PLO as its interlocutor in negotiations (contrary to popular belief, Israel never pledged to establish a Palestinian state at the outset of this process). Although the United States played no role in initiating the Oslo "peace process," President Bill Clinton presided over a gala signing

**Yitzhak Rabin, Bill Clinton, and Yasser Arafat during the Oslo Accords signing on 13 September 1993**

ceremony on the White House lawn in September 1993. Thereafter the United States played an exclusive role in overseeing and mediating the negotiations.

On that sun-dappled day, many believed that Bush's dream of a "new world order" was coming to fruition. The Soviet Union had imploded. Nelson Mandela was free from prison and the African National Congress was on the cusp of agreement with the South African government to end apartheid and transition to democracy. Britain was in secret talks with the Irish Republican Army, which led to a ceasefire and negotiations the next year over the fate of Northern Ireland. If these monumental transitions could occur, then couldn't Israeli-Palestinian peace be achieved as well? In recognition of the hope elicited by this agreement, Rabin, Foreign Minister Shimon Peres, and Arafat were jointly awarded the Nobel Peace Prize in 1994.

Israel and the PLO reached their first milestone in May 1994, agreeing to establish a Palestinian Authority (PA) with security forces to administer a limited degree of autonomy over Palestinians in parts of the West Bank and Gaza Strip. The ancient West Bank city of Jericho and 60 percent of the Gaza Strip (Israel retained full

## Economic Relations

In April 1994, Israel and the PLO signed the Paris Protocol, a document which set the terms for economic relations between the sides during the "peace process." The agreement largely codified Israel's existing dominance over the Palestinian economy, with Israel retaining the right to collect most taxes on behalf of the PA, keeping exclusive control over the currency, and overseeing Palestinian trade through control of border crossings while disallowing Palestinians from establishing independent means of importing and exporting.

control over the other 40 percent for its settlements and military bases there) were turned over to the PA as trial balloons. Arafat and the PLO leadership returned from exile to a tumultuous hero's reception in Gaza.

In September 1995, Israel and the PLO signed an agreement informally known as "Oslo II." The accord called for a series of phased redeployments of the Israeli military in the West Bank and carved the territory into three zones: In Area A, major Palestinian cities, the PA would exercise civil autonomy and assume day-to-day security control. In Area B, small Palestinian cities and villages, joint Israeli-Palestinian security patrols would be combined with the PA exercising civil autonomy in spheres such as education. In Area C, rural and uninhabited areas of the West Bank, Israel would keep full control. Israel's settlements, and East Jerusalem also remained under its exclusive jurisdiction. The resulting redeployments institutionalized islands of limited Palestinian autonomy within a sea of Israeli authority: Area A was 18 percent of the West Bank, Area B was 22 percent, and Area C was 60 percent.

Israel redeployed from most major Palestinian cities in the months both before and after Rabin's assassination by an Israeli Jewish religious extremist in November 1995, paving the way for the PA to hold presidential and legislative elections in January 1996, which resulted in a decisive win for Arafat and his Fatah party.

**UNITED NATIONS**
Office for the Coordination of Humanitarian Affairs, occupied Palestinian territory

## Restrictions on Palestinian Access in the West Bank          July 2011

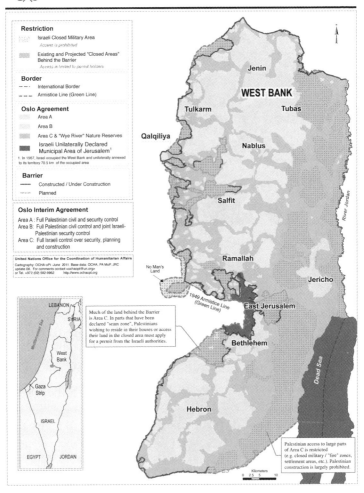

Despite these advances, Israeli-Palestinian relations were far from rosy and remained tenuous, characterized by mutual suspicions and recriminations. Israel had resumed its colonization of Palestinian land during the talks, prompting sentiments from Palestinians that it was negotiating in bad faith. Israel also began to slap long-term closures on the West Bank and Gaza Strip, inhibiting Palestinians from reaching their day laborer jobs in Israel and crippling the Palestinian economy. Israel's military also continued to injure and kill Palestinian civilians on a regular basis. In retaliation for an American-born Israeli settler massacring 29 Palestinians at prayer in a Hebron mosque in 1994, Hamas and other Palestinian groups outside the framework of the PLO launched a devastating rash of suicide bombings.

The "peace process" further lost momentum after Israel elected the right-wing Benjamin Netanyahu in its first-ever direct election for a prime minister in May 1996. Although Israel and the PLO signed the Hebron Protocol in January 1997, redeploying Israeli troops from 80 percent of the city while maintaining its soldiers in the remainder of the city to protect its small settlements there, and the Wye River Memorandum in October 1998, specifying further Israeli redeployments in the West Bank, Netanyahu stepped up the pace of Israeli settlement expansion and dithered on the implementation of agreed-upon redeployments. More important, Israel and the PLO never commenced negotiations on "final status" issues—the most nettlesome of the topics that divided Israel and the Palestinians, such as Jerusalem, refugees, water, settlements and borders. The Oslo accords had stipulated that these negotiations would begin no later than 1997 and conclude by 1999.

> **FACTS**
>
> President Bill Clinton chose Camp David as the site for Israeli-Palestinian "final status" talks because of its history in resolving the Arab-Israeli conflict. In 1978, President Jimmy Carter brokered Israeli-Egyptian accords at Camp David, which led to a peace treaty the following year.

The sputtering "peace process" was temporarily rejuvenated following the election of Ehud Barak as Israel's prime minister in May 1999. Barak pulled Israeli troops out of South Lebanon one year later, ending an 18-year military occupation there, and then plunged head-first into "final status" talks with the PLO, convincing Clinton to call for a summit meeting at Camp David to resolve all outstanding issues in one fell swoop. Arafat was reticent to attend a summit meeting, arguing that not enough preparatory work had been done yet to ensure success. He consented to attend, however, after Clinton promised him that no party would be blamed if the negotiations failed. The parties gathered for two intensive weeks of negotiations in July 2000.

For the first time, Israel put Palestinian statehood on the table. It was, however, a very truncated and circumscribed form of statehood. Although the Palestinian state would comprise more than 90 percent of the West Bank and all of Gaza, Israel would control its borders, airspace and water. Israel would annex its major settlement blocs in the West Bank, cutting the territory into a jigsaw-like puzzle piece and compensate the Palestinians with some barren, uninhabitable sand dunes appended to Gaza. Palestinians would have only limited autonomy, but no sovereignty, in East Jerusalem, including over their holy places, while Palestinian refugees would be denied their internationally recognized right of return. The Israeli offer was presented to the Palestinians in a take-it-or-leave-it fashion without

## Generous Offer?

Following the breakdown of the Camp David negotiations, Israeli and American officials roundly criticized Arafat for walking away from Barak's "generous offer." The mythology of Barak's "generous offer" played a significant role in Israel's marginalization of Arafat in the remaining years of his life. However, at least one Israeli official, former Foreign Minister Shlomo Ben-Ami, has noted, "If I were a Palestinian I would have rejected Camp David" too.

## The Palestine Papers

In 2011, a disgruntled member of the Palestinian negotiating team leaked 1,600 internal documents of "peace process" negotiations covering 1999 to 2010 to Al Jazeera. In one document, Tzipi Livni, a former foreign minister who was then the lead Israeli negotiator, attempted to convince her interlocutors to dispense with international law in the negotiations. "I am a lawyer… But I am against law—international law in particular. Law in general," she said, according to minutes of the talks.

official maps. Arafat, claiming that he would be assassinated if he accepted a deal so inimical to Palestinian rights, rejected it. The summit broke down in acrimony, and Clinton, despite his pledge to the contrary, placed the onus for failure solely on Arafat's shoulders.

A last-ditch attempt to salvage the "peace process" took place in Taba, Egypt, in January 2001. Although the negotiators issued a statement that they had "never been closer to reaching an agreement," it was too little, too late. Barak was a lame duck who was about to be steamrolled by Ariel Sharon in the February 2001 elections. Sharon, who had provocatively toured Muslim holy sites in Jerusalem with a thousand armed police in September 2000, touching off a second intifada against Israeli military occupation, came to power vowing to crush this uprising.

Sharon's five-year stint as prime minister was characterized by heavy-handed Israeli military repression, the marginalization of the PA as a "partner for peace," and unilateralism. Israel reinvaded and reoccupied Palestinian cities in the West Bank, built a wall deep into the West Bank, a move which the International Court of Justice declared illegal in July 2004, and besieged Arafat in his presidential compound in the Palestinian West Bank city of Ramallah until his death in November 2004. (Arafat was succeeded by his long-time deputy Mahmoud Abbas, who won the PA presidential election in January 2005.)

In August 2005, Israel unilaterally "disengaged" from the Gaza Strip by removing its small, illegal settlements and military bases from within Gaza while maintaining its control of the territory from without. Israel's dominance over Gaza's border crossings, territorial waters and airspace transformed into a full-fledged land, sea, and air blockade following Hamas's victory in the PA's legislative election in January 2006, the first election contested by this group, which had previously rejected participating in institutions established through the "peace process." Rather than engage Hamas in the political process, Israel and the United States, both of which characterize Hamas as a terrorist organization, immediately imposed sanctions on the new government and boycotted any dealings with it. The United States destabilized the situation further by providing support to train and equip new Palestinian security forces loyal to Fatah, which marched into Gaza from Egypt, triggering internecine fighting between it and Hamas. The struggle culminated in an intense battle in June 2007, in which Hamas routed Fatah. Despite several attempts at reconciliation since then, the rift between the two parties remains, leaving Palestinian politics in stasis.

In the summer of 2006, Israeli Prime Minister Ehud Olmert, who succeeded Sharon after the latter fell into a coma in January 2006, launched simultaneous attacks against the Gaza Strip and Lebanon after Hamas and Hezbollah military operations had

### Disengaging for Peace?

Israel often presents its unilateral disengagement from Gaza as a significant concession to advance Israeli-Palestinian peace. But according to Dov Weisglass, a senior adviser to Ariel Sharon, then Israel's prime minister, the intent of the plan was the exact opposite. "The significance of the disengagement plan is the freezing of the peace process," Weisglass stated. "This whole package called the Palestinian state...has been removed indefinitely from our agenda."

**FACTS**

Sheikh Ahmed Yassin, a paralyzed cleric who was assassinated by Israel in 2004, founded Hamas in the Gaza Strip in 1987. Hamas is an acronym for *Harakat al-Muqawamah al-Islamiyah*, or the Islamic Resistance Movement. Hamas also means "zeal" or "enthusiasm" in Arabic.

succeeded in taking captive several Israeli soldiers. In its attack on Lebanon, which killed an estimated 1,000 Lebanese civilians and destroyed billions of dollars of civilian infrastructure, the Israeli military first employed what it later termed the Dahiya Doctrine—the application of overwhelming and disproportionate force to deliberately target civilians and civilian infrastructure to compel political change, a clear breach of international law and a war crime. Israel would put this doctrine to devastating effect against the Gaza Strip in subsequent attacks.

The United States belatedly attempted to reverse this slide and reenergize the "peace process" by relaunching Israeli-Palestinian negotiations in Annapolis, Maryland, in November 2007. Talks continued through mid-2008 until Olmert resigned in the face of corruption charges, but the negotiations were bound to fail: the Israeli offer was only a slightly tweaked version of the rejected Camp David proposals. Again Israel offered the Palestinians no official map; instead, Abbas was relegated to sketching a map on a napkin outlining the proposal shown to him by Olmert.

Why was the Israeli-Palestinian "peace process," launched amid much fanfare in 1993, a dismal wreck fifteen years later? Beyond the day-to-day exchanges of violence and accusations, three primary reasons emerge. First, rather than end its colonization of Palestinian land, Israel used the negotiations as a cover for embarking on an unprecedented spree of settlement expansion. In this period, the population of Israeli settlers increased by 80 percent—from less than 300,000 to more than one-half million. The more Israel colonized this Palestinian land, the less likely were the odds that a viable and contiguous Palestinian state could emerge on it. Second, as the "peace process" limped along interminably, the PA became less of an interim administrative body and more of a permanent subcontractor in Israel's deepening military occupation of Palestinian land. The PA's existence allowed Israel to slough off its Fourth Geneva Convention obligations to provide for the needs of those under its occupation and instead made the Palestinians wards of the international community which bankrolled the PA. Third, when Israel intermittently submitted offers on "final status" issues to Palestinians, they were based not on UN resolutions and international law but rather on the strong attempting to dictate terms to the weak. All Israeli proposals fell well short of accommodating basic Palestinian human and national rights.

## Sources:

Robert Malley and Hussein Agha, "Camp David: The Tragedy of Errors," *New York Review of Books*, August 9, 2001, available at: http://www.nybooks.com/articles/archives/2001/aug/09/camp-david-the-tragedy-of-errors/

Israeli-Palestinian Joint Statement, January 27, 2001, available at: http://www.mideastweb.org/taba.htm

David Rose, "The Gaza Bombshell," *Vanity Fair*, April 2008, available at: http://www.vanityfair.com/news/2008/04/gaza200804

Gregg Carlstrom, "The 'napkin map' revealed," *Al Jazeera*, January 23, 2011, available at: http://www.aljazeera.com/palestinepapers/2011/01/2011122114239940577.html

"Comprehensive Settlement Population, 1972–2011," Foundation for Middle East Peace, available at: http://fmep.org/resource/comprehensive-settlement-population-1972-2010/

"Fmr. Israeli Foreign Minister: 'If I were a Palestinian, I Would Have Rejected Camp David,'" *Democracy Now,* February 4, 2006, available at http://www.democracynow.org/2006/2/14/fmr_israeli_foreign_minister_if_i

"Livni: A lawyer 'against law'?," *Al-Jazeera*, January 24, 2011, available at http://www.aljazeera.com/palestinepapers/2011/01/2011124165334291715.html

Ari Shavit, ""Top PM Aide: Gaza Plan Aims to Freeze the Peace Process," Haaretz, October 6, 2004, available at, http://www.haaretz.com/print-edition/news/top-pm-aide-gaza-plan-aims-to-freeze-the-peace-process-1.136686

**US Secretary of State John Kerry, Israeli Prime Minister Benjamin
Netanyahu Make Press Statements, September 2013**

# Israel's Prime Minister: Benjamin Netanyahu

Move over David Ben-Gurion. The iconic first prime minister of Israel now shares the record with Benjamin Netanyahu, the current Israeli prime minister, for most terms (four) served at the helm of the Israeli government. And if Netanyahu's governing coalition holds together for its full term, then by 2019 he will have served as prime minister for ten consecutive years—the longest streak in Israel's history. Born in 1949, Netanyahu is Israel's first prime minister born after the establishment of the state.

Netanyahu first rose to prominence in the 1980s as Israel's ambassador to the UN. His fluent command of English—parts of his childhood and his high school and college education were spent in the United States—made him a favorite of the US media. In 1988, Netanyahu returned to Israel, joined the hard-line Likud party and first won election to Israel's parliament—the Knesset—where he served as deputy foreign minister.

After Likud was defeated by Labor in Israel's 1992 elections, Netanyahu was elected as his party's leader, injecting a fresh face into what had become a stultifying leadership. In his role as opposition leader, he published a book, *A Place Among the Nations*, in which he strenuously argued against turning land over to the Palestinians. This manifesto would serve as a blueprint for his first term as prime minister (1996–1999) as he ground the Oslo "peace process" to a halt.

After losing to Ehud Barak in the 1999 election, Netanyahu temporarily retired from politics. He became foreign minister in Ariel Sharon's government in 2002 but his political reemergence appeared permanently stymied after failing to dislodge Sharon from the party's leadership position later that year. His fortunes brightened after Sharon bolted Likud to form a new party, allowing Netanyahu to recapture the party's leadership in 2005 and the prime ministerial post four years later.

Palestinian Authority President Mahmoud Abbas, May 23, 2017

# Palestinian Authority President Mahmoud Abbas

Mahmoud Abbas was born in 1935 in Safed in the Galilee region of northern Palestine and fled to Syria with his family during the *Nakba*, the Palestinian term for the destruction of their society which resulted from the establishment of Israel. Abbas, also known as Abu Mazen, worked for the Qatari civil service in the 1950s and while in Qatar became involved in Palestinian politics and became an early member of Yasser Arafat's Fatah party in 1961. Fatah later became the dominant political party in the Palestine Liberation Organization.

Within the PLO, Abbas was an early advocate for holding talks with Israel, and in 1993 he signed the Declaration of Principles, which initiated the Israeli-Palestinian peace process, on behalf of the PLO. The peace process established the Palestinian Authority (PA) to implement limited autonomy for Palestinians in the West Bank and Gaza Strip. Arafat, the PA's first president, appointed Abbas prime minister in 2003.

Abbas became acting president of the PA upon Arafat's death in 2004, and in 2005 he was elected to the position for a four-year term. In 2006, Hamas won the Palestinian legislative elections, leading to a mini-civil war between it and Fatah, which effectively bifurcated the PA into two administrations, with Hamas running the PA in Gaza and Abbas's Fatah party retaining control of the PA in the West Bank.

Despite several subsequent attempts to reunify the PA, this polarization has solidified, leading to a stasis in Palestinian politics. Abbas unilaterally extended his term by one year after it was supposed to have expired in 2009. Today, many Palestinians view him as a leader lacking a mandate who has no coherent plan to achieve Palestinian rights. His boldest initiative was a bid in 2011 to have Palestine become a full member of the UN, a move which was stymied due to US opposition.

# "A Strategic Threat of the Highest Degree"

It represents "a strategic threat of the highest degree," warned Israel's president, Reuven Rivlin, in 2015. And Israel's government has appointed a high-level task force overseen by its minister of strategic affairs to combat it, spending approximately $25 million annually to do so.

This strategic threat is not a new advanced missile system acquired by Hezbollah or Hamas. It is not the development of nuclear warfighting capabilities by one its stated adversaries. Instead, this strategic threat to Israel comes from an initiative of Palestinian civil society calling for nonviolent campaigns of boycott, divestment and sanctions (BDS) against Israel and companies and institutions which enable its oppression of Palestinians.

In 2005, more than 170 Palestinian political parties, trade unions, women's rights organizations and grassroots and nongovernmental organizations launched an international call for these BDS campaigns to leverage pressure to compel Israel to end its military occupation of territories it conquered in 1967, to end its discriminatory laws, which make Palestinian citizens of Israel second-class citizens, and to enable Palestinian refugees to exercise their right of return.

This global call for BDS campaigns was issued by the Palestinian BDS National Committee on the one-year anniversary of the International Court of Justice (ICJ) issuing its advisory opinion that the wall Israel has built in the West Bank is illegal and must be torn down. In light of the fact that Israel has failed to comply with this ruling and that foreign governments also have turned a blind eye to the ICJ's ruling that countries cannot render aid or assistance to Israel to maintain the wall, the Palestinian-led BDS movement is a global call to conscience for concerned people to take action themselves when governments have manifestly failed to uphold their duties under international law.

Arguing that "Israel maintains a regime of settler colonialism, apartheid and occupation over the Palestinian people," the BDS movement draws inspiration from and models itself after the global campaign that played such a prominent role in forcing South Africa to dismantle its separate-and-unequal system of racial discrimination.

Israel's response to the BDS movement recalls a pithy theory of the stages of social change often attributed to, but apparently never actually said by, Mahatma Gandhi: "First they ignore you, then they laugh at you, then they fight you, then you win." If this sequencing holds true for the attainment of Palestinian rights, then upholders of Israel's discriminatory regime do indeed have reason to treat the BDS movement as a strategic threat. Within the span of little more than a decade, the BDS movement has become a global phenomenon, racking up impressive support from trade unions, student governments, academic associations and pension funds worldwide, and generating enough pressure on multinational corporations to withdraw from projects in which they formerly profited from Israel's military occupation. Israel's early dismissal of the import of the BDS movement appears in hindsight to have been a mistake; its attempts today to combat it seem to be rearguard actions that have failed to stem the momentum of the movement.

The BDS movement has had a major impact on the bottom line of corporations that increasingly have been extricating themselves from involvement in Israeli military occupation rather than suffer ongoing reputational risk as the targets of global boycott campaigns. The French company Veolia learned this lesson the hard way. As a result of profiting from waste management and transportation contracts servicing Israel's illegal settlements in the Palestinian West Bank, Veolia lost an estimated $20 billion in potential contracts worldwide as a globally coordinated boycott campaign successfully pressured municipalities and national governments to exclude the company from bidding. Veolia executives admitted that the BDS campaign cost the company "important contracts." The company hurriedly made a complete exit from the Israeli market in 2015 after selling off the last of its stakes in projects there, a five percent share in the Jerusalem Light Rail, a project that integrates Israel's illegal settlements in East Jerusalem with the city's western sector.

Israeli companies—especially those based in or tied to illegal Israeli settlements—have also faced negative economic repercussions when challenged by the BDS movement. In 2011, Agrexco, an Israeli agriculture exporter partially subsidized by the government, was forced into liquidation after being unable to pay its debts. Prior to its liquidation, Agrexco was the company responsible for marketing an estimated 60–70 percent of agricultural produce from Israeli settlements. The company lost substantial revenue after becoming a target of a continental BDS boycott campaign in Europe, where grassroots coalitions succeeded in removing Agrexco products from supermarkets in Italy and the United Kingdom.

Another Israeli company forced to upend its business model as a direct result of BDS campaigning is SodaStream, which manufactures a formerly popular carbonation device for making soda at home. SodaStream's primary manufacturing plant was located in the Israeli settlement of Mishor Adumim in the West Bank where it operated on expropriated Palestinian land and exploited a captive Palestinian labor market suffering under Israel's deliberate policies to de-develop the local economy. SodaStream's sales and stock value plummeted as BDS campaigns succeeded in getting retailers such as Macy's to drop the product and investors such as the Soros Management Fund to divest their holdings. The BDS movement's ability to cause reputational damage to the company by linking the company's profits to Israel's illegal settlements forced the company to move its main manufacturing plant to Israel. SodaStream, however, remains a target of the BDS movement because its new manufacturing plant in Israel is located near Rahat, a community being built by Israel to forcibly transfer its Bedouin citizens to make room for Jewish-only settlements in the area.

Perhaps most worrisome to Israel and its supporters is the growing success that BDS campaigns are having in the United States.

Israel has long considered the strong support for Palestinian rights in the developing world, and to a lesser extent in Europe, to be manageable as long as it could rely on the steadfast support of the United States. However, the nearly unanimous support Israel once enjoyed from US civil society is unraveling as BDS gains traction.

Many mainstream church denominations representing tens of millions of Americans—including the United Methodist Church and Presbyterian Church (USA)—have voted to boycott Israeli settlement products, divested church monies from US corporations and Israeli banks profiting from Israel's occupation, and have called upon the US government to end weapons transfers to Israel. Major musical performers such as Lauryn Hill, The Killers, Carlos Santana, and Talib Kweli, have canceled concerts in Israel in response to BDS campaigns, and Stevie Wonder canceled a benefit performance in the United States for an organization providing funds to the Israeli military. In addition, dozens of student governments on campuses throughout the country have called upon their university administrations to divest school money from companies profiting from Israeli occupation, and several prominent academic associations, such as the American Anthropological Association, the American Studies Association, and the Critical Ethnic Studies Associations, have passed BDS resolutions or adopted a boycott of Israeli academic institutions.

These impressive BDS victories in the United States have triggered a furious legislative backlash by state legislators and members of Congress who support Israel's oppressive policies toward Palestinians. According to Palestine Legal, dozens of anti-BDS bills and resolutions have been introduced in state houses since 2014, and as of May 2017, 19 states have enacted anti-BDS legislation. These initiatives range from resolutions condemning the BDS movement and its goals to bills that divest state pension funds from companies that support BDS to bills that proscribe state contracts from being awarded to companies or institutions that support BDS. A bill introduced in Congress in 2017—the Israel Anti-Boycott Act—even seeks to impose criminal penalties on corporations advancing the goals of international boycotts against Israeli settlement products.

Many of these pieces of anti-BDS legislation appear to be of dubious constitutional validity as they seek to impose governmental sanctions on companies and institutions for exercising their freedom of expression. The Supreme Court has maintained that these types of campaigns are forms of political speech, and that "speech on public issues occupies the highest rung of the hierarchy of First Amendment values, and is entitled to special protection." These desperate attempts to suppress the BDS movement through legislative means appear not only to be unconstitutional but to be counterproductive as well. BDS campaigns continue to proliferate, and support for sanctioning Israel is gaining mainstream acceptance in the United States. According to a November 2016 poll by the Brookings Institution, 46 percent of all Americans and 60 percent of Democrats want the United States to impose economic sanctions on Israel to stop its expansion of illegal settlements. Continuing inroads by the BDS movement in the United States could inevitably undermine the current US governmental support Israel enjoys for its policies toward Palestinians, making them unsustainable in the future.

## SOURCES:

Michael Omer-Man, "Israel's president calls BDS a 'strategic threat'," *+972 Magazine*, May 28, 2015, available at: https://972mag.com/israels-president-says-bds-is-a-strategic-threat/107156/

Doron Peskin, "Israel commits $25 million to new anti-BDS task force, but what exactly will they do?" *Al-Monitor*, December 23, 2015, available at: http://www.al-monitor.com/pulse/originals/2015/12/boycott-bds-movement-israel-government-office-gilad-erdan.html

"What Is BDS?" Palestinian BDS National Committee, available at: https://bdsmovement.net/what-is-bds

Dan Evon, "First They Ignore You, Then They Vote for You?" *Snopes*, March 1, 2016, available at: http://www.snopes.com/first-they-ignore-you/

"BDS marks another victory as Veolia sells off all Israeli operations," Palestinian BDS National Committee, September 1, 2015, available at: https://bdsmovement.net/news/bds-marks-another-victory-veolia-sells-all-israeli-operations

"Palestinian civil society welcomes Agrexco liquidation, calls for celebration of this BDS victory," Palestinian BDS National Committee, September 12, 2011, available at: https://bdsmovement.net/news/palestinian-civil-society-welcomes-agrexco-liquidation-calls-celebration-bds-victory

"SodaStream to close illegal settlement factory in response to growing boycott campaign," Palestinian BDS National Committee, October 30, 2014, available at: https://bdsmovement.net/news/sodastream-close-illegal-settlement-factory-response-growing-boycott-campaign

"UPATED: List of 200+ US BDS Victories!," US Campaign for Palestinian Rights, May 14, 2017, available at: https://uscpr.org/usbdsvictories/

"Anti-BDS Legislation by State," Palestine Legal, available at: http://righttoboycott.org/

"Palestine Legal's Statement Re: Calls to Ban SJP from CUNY campuses," November 20, 2015, Palestine Legal, available at: http://palestinelegal.org/news/2015/11/20/statement-re-calls-to-ban-students-for-justice-in-palestine-sjp-from-city-university-of-new-york-cuny

Shibley Telhami, "American attitudes on the Israeli-Palestinian conflict," December 2, 2016, Brookings, available at: https://www.brookings.edu/research/american-attitudes-on-the-israeli-palestinian-conflict/

# US-Israel Relations

"Shared values" between the United States and Israel "compel us to reaffirm that our enduring friendship with the people of Israel and our unbreakable bonds with the state of Israel—that those bonds, that friendship cannot be broken," stated President Barack Obama in May 2015. "Our commitment to Israel's security…is and always will be unshakeable."

Despite the often frosty personal relations that existed between Obama and Israeli Prime Minister Benjamin Netanyahu, these sentiments are an accurate indication of the extraordinary degree to which the United States has backed Israel, both diplomatically and militarily. Since 1972, the United States has used its veto power in the UN Security Council on more than 40 occasions to prevent the international body from condemning Israel's policies. And in 2015, the United States provided Israel with $3.1 billion in military aid—more than all other countries in the world combined.

How did US-Israel relations come to be so "unbreakable" and "unshakeable"? What accounts for the exceptional degree of closeness between the two countries today? Will the same relationship prevail in the future?

The United States played a seminal role in Israel's establishment in 1948. It backed the UN Partition Plan and leaned heavily on other countries to endorse the creation of a Jewish state in Palestine. Despite recognizing Israel just eleven minutes after the country's declaration of independence, President Harry Truman had deep misgivings over Israel's role in creating the Palestinian refugee crisis. Truman placed an arms embargo on Israel and neighboring Arab states, and in 1950 joined with Great Britain and France in the Tripartite Declaration to prevent a regional arms race. In its early years, Israel was primarily considered a charity case by the United

States: from 1949 to 1965, more than 95 percent of US assistance to Israel was in the form of food aid and economic development.

During these years, the United States was much more willing than today to leverage its considerable pressure over Israel to obtain its foreign policy objectives. Under President Dwight Eisenhower, the United States sanctioned Israel twice. In 1953, it suspended aid to compel Israel to end a hyrdroelectric dam project, which diverted water from its neighbors. In 1956, the United States again froze aid to force Israel to withdraw from its military occupation of the Egyptian Sinai Peninsula following a joint Israeli-British-French attack. Eisenhower even threatened that he would prohibit private US charity from reaching Israel if it did not leave Egypt; Israel announced its withdrawal the next day.

Despite these strains in the bilateral relationship under Eisenhower, in 1959 his administration provided Israel with its first modest military aid loan, of $400,000. Under the Kennedy administration, Israel obtained its first advanced weapons—Hawk anti-aircraft missiles—from the United States. Weapons from the United States continued to flow to Israel, but President Lyndon Johnson publicly worried about the consequences of Israel's territorial aggrandizement in the aftermath of the 1967 Arab-Israeli war. He warned that Israel should not "permit military success to blind it to the fact that its neighbors have rights" and condemned the "waste and futility" of an Arab-Israeli arms race. His administration sponsored UN Security Council Resolution 242, calling for Israel's withdrawal from territories it occupied in this war.

**DID YOU KNOW?**

Israel is the largest recipient of US foreign assistance in the post-World War II era. From 1949 to 2008, the United States gave Israel $103.6 billion of military and economic aid. In the period from 2009 to 2028, the United States is scheduled to give Israel as much as $68 billion in weapons.

President Richard Nixon paid no heed to his predecessor's warning, especially during and after the 1973 Arab-Israeli war. Emergency airlifts of US weapons to Israel were credited with saving it from defeat. The next year, the United States gave Israel $2.5 billion in military aid loans and, for the first time, military aid grants to replenish the weapons it used in the war, ushering in the present era of largesse, which has made Israel the largest cumulative recipient of US aid since World War II.

The Israeli-Egyptian peace treaty, signed in 1979 under the patronage of President Jimmy Carter, institutionalized ever-deepening amounts of US assistance to Israel. Carter pledged a whopping $4 billion in military aid loans and grants to Israel. Thereafter, the United States began negotiating memoranda of understanding with Israel setting out the terms of US assistance in ten-year increments, a practice which continues today. In 1985, President Ronald Reagan ended loans to Israel and converted all US assistance into nonrepayable grants.

Under President Bill Clinton, the United States and Israel agreed to do away with economic assistance while at the same time increasing military aid. President George W. Bush increased the amount of weapons provided to Israel even further, pledging $30 billion from 2009 to 2018. In 2016, the Obama administration signed a deal to provide Israel $38 billion in additional weapons in the subsequent decade.

At least three factors account for the singular relationship the United States has with Israel today. First and foremost, the existence of the well-oiled and well-funded Israel lobby plays a major role in ensuring ongoing, nearly unconditional US diplomatic and military support for Israel. To speak of the Israel lobby's role in setting the agenda

---

From 2000 to 2009, the United States gave Israel more than $24 billion in military aid, which paid for the delivery to Israel of more than 670 million weapons and rounds of ammunition.

**FACTS**

for the US-Israel relationship is not an exercise in dark, conspiratorial thinking. On the contrary, the dozens, perhaps hundreds, of US-based organizations—both Jewish-American and Christian Zionist—which advocate for Israel are quite open about their objectives. The American Israel Public Affairs Committee, for example, sends thousands of citizen lobbyists to Capitol Hill every year to advocate for more weapons to Israel. In addition, individual Zionists such as Sheldon Adelson and Haim Saban are major donors to the Republican and Democratic Parties, respectively—and their congressional and presidential candidates—ensuring that both major parties toe the line. While the Israel lobby's ability to dictate the contours of US policy toward Israel and the Palestinians is largely unassailable, its power to control broader US foreign policy is questionable as demonstrated by its failure to stop the 2015 Iran nuclear deal.

## "I know what America is. America is something that can be moved easily." —Benjamin Netanyahu, Israeli prime minister

Second, the United States derives considerable benefit from its military relationship with Israel. Israel is the only country in the world that can spend US military aid (up to 26 percent of the total) on its own domestic arms industry. This added bonus amounts to US taxpayers providing the Israeli arms industry with an annual $800 million subsidy at current levels. This subsidy has helped launch Israel into the top tier of weapons exporters in its own right. Israel is now the world's fifth-largest arms exporter. Its military-industrial corporations collaborate with US weapons manufactures on the development of key weapons systems. For example, Israel Aerospace Industries and Elbit, respectively, provide avionics for the next-generation F-35 fighter jet and computing capabilities for Bradley Fighting Vehicles.

Third, as a country also founded on the dispossession and ethnic cleansing of its indigenous population, the United States does indeed "share values" with Israel. The US drive across the continent in the nineteenth century resulted in the forced removal of indigenous populations and their confinement to ever-shrinking "reservations" of land. The United States repeatedly broke its treaty obligations with indigenous nations to take additional land as it saw fit. What the United States did to its indigenous population, Israel continues to do to Palestinians today.

Israel also benefits politically from the deep reservoir of religious support it is able to draw from in the United States. Many religious and secular Jewish-Americans view political backing for Israel as a quasi-religious obligation, although today more are openly questioning its policies. And tens of millions of voters identify as Christian Zionists, constituting a powerful voting bloc. The more extreme of these adherents faithfully lobby for a militaristic Israel whose warfare, in their eschatological view, will trigger Armageddon and the second coming of Jesus.

Israel has traditionally relied on bipartisan comity to assure its "special relationship" with the United States. However, that comity is fraying as Israel is becoming a partisan issue on Capitol Hill. In March 2015, Netanyahu delivered a controversial address to Congress attempting to undercut what would become Obama's signature foreign policy accomplishment: the nuclear deal with Iran. His speech, engineered with then-House Speaker John Boehner, behind the president's back, infuriated many Democrats, leading to one-quarter of the party's caucus boycotting it.

This unprecedented partisan breach is reflected in recent public opinion polls as well. For example, a December 2014 poll found a "wide gap" between the parties' respective bases on the Israeli-Palestinian issue, with 51 percent of Republicans wanting the United States to lean toward Israel and only 17 percent of Democrats agreeing. The same poll found significant support for Palestinians among youth, African-Americans and Hispanics, all of which are increasingly important Democratic voting blocs, suggesting "that this gap may grow further" in the future. While US support for Israel is currently rock-solid, and these shifts among the Democratic Party's base have not yet translated to change on

Capitol Hill, this growing partisan gap could erode US support for Israel down the road.

> **FACTS**
>
> By a 44 to 37 percent margin, Hispanic-Americans favor imposing economic sanctions on Israel for its settlement building more than non-Hispanic-Americans. Twelve percent of Hispanics rate the Israeli-Palestinian issue as their top foreign policy concern; only 4 percent of non-Hispanics agree.

## Sources:

Gideon Levy, ""Tricky Bibi," Haaretz, July 15, 2010, available at http://www.haaretz.com/print-edition/opinion/tricky-bibi-1.302053

"Remarks by the President on Jewish American Heritage Month,"The White House, May 22, 2015, available at: https://obamawhitehouse.archives.gov/the-press-office/2015/05/22/remarks-president-jewish-american-heritage-month

U.N. Security Council: U.S. Vetoes of Resolutions Critical to Israel (1972 - Present), Jewish Virtual Library, available at: https://www.jewishvirtu-allibrary.org/jsource/UN/usvetoes.html

Josh Ruebner, "U.S. Military Aid to Israel: Policy Implications & Options," US Campaign to End the Israeli Occupation, March 2012.

Josh Ruebner, Shattered Hopes: Obama's Failure to Broker Israeli-Palestinian Peace, Verso, 2014, p. 180.

Shibley Telhami and Katayoun Kishi, "Widening Democratic Party divisions on the Israeli-Palestinian issue," Washington Post, December 15, 2014, available at: https://www.wash-ingtonpost.com/blogs/monkey-cage/wp/2014/12/15/widening-democratic-party-divisions-on-the-israeli-palestinian-issue/

## Will Trump Secure the "Ultimate Deal"?

Donald Trump has referred to the prospect of brokering Israeli-Palestinian peace as the "ultimate deal" and, at the outset of his administration, has placed it high on his foreign policy agenda. In the first few months of his presidency, Trump separately invited Israeli Prime Minister Benjamin Netanyahu and Palestinian Authority President Mahmoud Abbas for high-profile White House visits. The Israeli and Palestinian leaders reciprocated when Trump visited both Israel and the occupied Palestinian West Bank as part of his first presidential trip abroad in May 2017. At each opportunity, Trump has indicated his eagerness to restart the Israeli-Palestinian peace process and appears to have confidence in his ability to resolve an issue that has stymied all of his predecessors in the White House since Harry Truman recognized Israel in 1948. After emerging from his first meeting with Abbas, Trump declaimed that the Israeli-Palestinian issue is "something that I think is, frankly, maybe not as difficult as people have thought over the years."

As a real estate tycoon and author of *The Art of the Deal*, Trump has styled himself as a consummate businessman with a razor-sharp acumen for negotiations. Is his self-assurance in his ability to bring about Israeli-Palestinian peace warranted, or will the neophyte politician discover to his chagrin, as he did on health care reform, that "it's an unbelievably complex subject" which "nobody knew... could be so complicated"?

Unlike Barack Obama, who entered the White House "unbelievably informed" about the Israeli-Palestinian issue, according to Netanyahu, Trump had little relevant experience on foreign policy issues in general and on Israeli-Palestinian issues in particular, save for a brief business trip to Israel in 1989, before he became president. Making Trump an even more unlikely personage to assume the role of unbiased facilitator of Israeli-Palestinian peace is the fact that the entirety of his pre-presidential engagement on this issue was filtered through the prism of family members and lawyers on his payroll, all of whom are intimately connected to and, in some cases, personally identified with Israel's colonization of Palestinian land.

Trump's son-in-law, Jared Kushner, has assumed a jack-of-all-trades role in the White House with a multiplicity of portfolios assigned to him as the president's senior adviser, including negotiating Israeli-Palestinian peace. Although Kushner's views on this subject are not widely known and his peers from high school and college describe him as largely apolitical, his family's close connections to Israel and his upbringing in religious Jewish schools imbued with Zionist worldviews would appear to raise questions about his partiality. Not only has his family heavily invested in Israeli real estate projects, but its family foundation has donated money to organizations funneling money to Israeli settlements, and Kushner himself served on the board of Friends of the Israeli Defense Forces, a US organization which raises money for the Israeli military. His family is so close to Netanyahu that the prime minister once slept in Kushner's childhood bedroom in New Jersey.

Trump has tapped Jason Greenblatt, his former real estate lawyer, to be his special representative for international negotiations, and in this role Greenblatt has been shuttling between Israeli and Palestinian officials to lay the groundwork for the resumption of negotiations. In the 1980s, Greenblatt studied at a Jewish religious institution in an Israeli settlement in the West Bank; he pulled guard duty there while studying, armed with an M16. Prior to his appointment by Trump, Greenblatt confessed that his only previous interactions with any Palestinians were informal ones with day laborers in the settlement and nearby store owners.

The most controversial figure among the leading triumvirate of Trump's advisers on the Israeli-Palestinian issue is his former bankruptcy lawyer David Friedman, whom Trump appointed to be US ambassador to Israel. Friedman served as the president of a nonprofit organization which raised millions of dollars to support the Israeli settlement of Beit El, located on expropriated Palestinian land near Ramallah. As a regular columnist for *Arutz Sheva*, a media outlet closely aligned with Israel's settler movement, Friedman regularly fulminated against Palestinian statehood and referred to the West Bank by its biblical names, claiming that "this is our land." He also excoriated Jewish people who opposed Israel's colonization of Palestinian land, describing them as being "far worse than kapos," a term for Jews who were coerced into collaborating with the Nazis. In March 2017, his nomination squeaked through the Senate in an extremely close, largely partisan vote.

During the 2016 presidential campaign, Friedman and Greenblatt served as the cochairs of Trump's Israel Advisory Committee (the campaign dispensed with any pretense that it was even nominally interested in being advised on Palestinian issues), guiding the most one-sided approach a presidential candidate has ever taken on the issue. With the Trump campaign's approval, the Republican Party dropped support for Palestinian statehood from its platform, which had been a consistent plank since the George W. Bush presidency. Instead, the GOP adopted language which would allow Israel to unilaterally impose dictated terms of surrender to the Palestinians. In addition, the Trump campaign raised the expectations of the Israeli right wing to a frenzy by promising to be sympathetic to Israel's colonization of Palestinian land and vowing to move the US embassy to Jerusalem and recognize the contested city as Israel's undivided capital. These pledges, if implemented, would reverse decades of bipartisan US policy opposing Israeli settlements and withholding recognition of claims to sovereignty over Jerusalem until after a peace agreement is concluded.

Given the backgrounds of Trump's key Israel advisers and the extravagant commitments he made on the campaign trail, it is small wonder that Israel's right wing feels bewildered, if not completely let down, by the president's apparent reversal of his stands at the outset of his administration. Rather than allow Israel an unfettered hand to colonize the West Bank, Trump publicly called on Netanyahu to "hold back on settlements for a little bit," as his administration engaged in inconclusive talks with Israel in an attempt to find a mutually agreeable geographical scope for further settlement expansion. Trump has also walked back his formerly vociferous support for moving the US embassy to Jerusalem, acknowledging that to do so would scupper any chance of resuming negotiations. In June 2017, Trump quietly signed an extension of a presidential waiver that must be renewed every six months to keep the US embassy in Tel Aviv, according to the terms of the Jerusalem Embassy Act, passed by Congress in 1995.

Will Trump's backpedaling on Israeli settlements and Jerusalem, combined with the unexpectedly warm rapport he has developed with Abbas (to Netanyahu's great angst), translate into an ability to clinch the "ultimate deal" and inaugurate Israeli-Palestinian peace? The answer is likely no. While conjecturing that Israeli-Palestinian peace could be far easier to achieve than many believe, Trump's hypothesis remains untested as he has brought no concrete ideas for how to restart negotiations, much less shepherd them to a successful conclusion. And his legendarily short attention span and unwillingness to delve into the depth of policy issues would seem to preclude him from assuming the type of role played by Bill Clinton, who famously pored over the minutia of maps with Israeli and Palestinian negotiators and expended tremendous amounts of political capital in his failed bid to attain this elusive goal.

Even if Trump evinced a proclivity for investing the time and prestige it would take to negotiate a deal, his approach to peacemaking would still be constrained by the worldview of his advisers. Ever since Clinton initiated the domineering US role in the Israeli-Palestinian peace process, most of the key US officials—with a brief interlude at the outset of the Obama administration being an exception to the rule—working on this issue came from a distinctly pro-Israel ideological bent. The members of Trump's team are not only pro-Israel but solidly pro-right-wing Israel, making them even less inclined to support Palestinian rights than previous US negotiators, who often showed disdain toward Palestinian aspirations. This perhaps explains why Trump has dropped support for Palestinian statehood from his public pronouncements on the issue and failed to express support for Palestinian self-determination when he met with Abbas in Bethlehem.

To the extent that Trump has crystallized any notions of how to attain Middle East peace, he appears to have endorsed Netanyahu's belief that a broader Arab-Israeli peace can be established to create a joint front to confront Iran's regional ambitions. In Netanyahu's eyes, this deal can be achieved by placating Palestinians with economic inducements while sidestepping their political rights. This, however, is not a viable plan for Israeli-Palestinian peace, but a blueprint for Israel's perpetual domination over the Palestinians.

## SOURCES:

Brian Bennett and Tracy Wilkinson, "Trump's approach to an Israeli-Palestinian peace deal: Get to yes, and figure out the details later," *Los Angeles Times*, May 3, 2017, available at: http://www.latimes.com/politics/la-fg-trump-abbas-20170503-story.html

Kevin Liptak, "Trump: 'Nobody knew health care could be so complicated'," CNN, February 28, 2017, available at: http://www.cnn.com/2017/02/27/politics/trump-health-care-complicated/

Josh Ruebner, *Shattered Hopes: Obama's Failure to Broker Israeli-Palestinian Peace*, Verso, 2014, p. 27

Jodi Kantor, "For Kushner, Israel Policy May Be Shaped by the Personal," *New York Times*, February 11, 2017, available at: https://www.nytimes.com/2017/02/11/us/politics/jared-kushner-israel.html

Uriel Hielman, "No experience necessary: Meet the Orthodox lawyer advising Trump on Israel," *Jewish Telegraphic Agency*, April 18, 2016, available at: http://www.jta.org/2016/04/18/news-opinion/politics/no-experience-necessary-meet-the-orthodox-lawyer-advising-trump-on-israel

"Oppose Nomination of David Friedman to Be Ambassador to Israel: Our Ambassador Must Represent US Interests, Not Israeli Settlers," US Campaign for Palestinian Rights, available at: https://uscpr.org/campaign/government-affairs/resources/oppose-friedman-nomination/

"Remarks by President Trump and Prime Minister Netanyahu of Israel in Joint Press Conference," White House, Office of the Press Secretary, February 15, 2017, available at: https://www.whitehouse.gov/the-press-office/2017/02/15/remarks-president-trump-and-prime-minister-netanyahu-israel-joint-press

# Israel and the Palestinians: Headed to Where?

In recent years, the probability of a negotiated, two-state resolution to the Israeli-Palestinian issue has gone from slim to virtually nonexistent.

Israel has kept the Gaza Strip under stringent lock and key, enforcing a blockade that denies Palestinians access to adequate levels of food and medicine. Regular Israeli military incursions into the Gaza Strip, along with the exchange of fire between Israel and armed Palestinian groups, have precipitated three large-scale Israeli attacks on the Gaza Strip: Operations Cast Lead (2008–2009), Pillar of Defense (2012), and Protective Edge (2014). Ostensibly designed to suppress Palestinian rocket and mortar fire into Israel, these Israeli attacks have served as ghastly applications of the Dahiyeh Doctrine—employing overwhelming and disproportionate force targeting civilians and pulverizing civilian infrastructure. According to the UN and Palestinian and Israeli human rights organizations, Israel killed more than 3,700 Palestinians in these attacks, nearly three-fourths of whom were civilians, including more than 800 children. In the most recent attack alone, Israel damaged or destroyed 18,000 houses, rendering more than 100,000 Palestinians homeless. Because of Israel's blockade, it is virtually impossible for Palestinians to rebuild their homes, despite the international community pledging billions of dollars to reconstruct Gaza. The UN has warned that

**FACTS**

Palestinians in the blockaded Gaza Strip lack access to clean drinking water. Between 90 and 95 percent of Gaza's underground water aquifer is unpotable and unfit for agricultural use, in part because it has been contaminated due to Israel's bombing of wastewater treatment facilities.

Gaza may be "uninhabitable" by 2020 due to a combination of the effects of Israel's blockade and attacks and Palestinian population growth in what is already one of the most densely populated places on earth.

Meanwhile in the West Bank, Israel has continued to colonize Palestinian land at an unabated pace. As of 2015, approximately 650,000 Israeli settlers lived in the West Bank, including East Jerusalem, among less than three million Palestinians, balkanizing Palestinian land into ever shrinking enclaves. In 2013, Israel announced plans to build a train network connecting West Bank Palestinian cities and Israeli settlements to Israel, signifying its long-term intent to retain control over these Palestinian territories and integrate them into Israel. Israeli Prime Minister Benjamin Netanyahu won reelection in March 2015 in large measure by vowing that a Palestinian state would never be established on his watch.

## "The settlement movement…may well drive Israel into an irreversible binational reality." –Ambassador Martin Indyk, US Special Envoy for Israeli-Palestinian Negotiations, May 2014

As the sponsor of the Israeli-Palestinian "peace process," officially wedded to a two-state resolution since Bill Clinton adopted it in the waning months of his administration, the United States has tried to salvage its prospects while warning Israel that time is running out. Barack Obama entered the White House in 2009, intent on brokering Israeli-Palestinian peace and confident in his ability to do so. His unwillingness to use US leverage to compel Israel to freeze its settlement building resulted in a short-lived round of talks in September 2010. From July 2013 to April 2014, Secretary of State John Kerry did succeed in getting negotiators back to the table, presiding over the most intensive series of talks between the sides since 2008. However, the negotiations predictably foundered as the United States backed Israel's warmed-over

> **Two-state solution**: Establishing a Palestinian state next to Israel.
>
> **One-state solution:** Palestinians and Israelis Jews living as equals in the same democratic structure.

**GLOSSARY**

proposals to annex most major Israeli settlements, retain control over Palestinian border crossings and airspace, deny Palestinian sovereignty in Jerusalem and prevent Palestinian refugees from returning.

These negotiations were the desperate, last-ditch efforts of the United States to establish a Palestinian state. In April 2013, Kerry had recognized that time was of the essence, testifying to Congress that there was at most a two-year window of opportunity for creating a Palestinian state before Israel's colonization of Palestinian land rendered the concept irrelevant.

With the prospects for a two-state solution virtually dead and buried, what does the future portend for Israel and the Palestinians and what other options exist to resolve the issues between them?

Israel's preferred option appears to be to maintain the status quo for as long as possible, continuing its military occupation of the Palestinian West Bank and Gaza Strip indefinitely while colonizing the former and blockading the latter. Here the law of inertia dominates Israeli decision-making: one-half century of military occupation has inured the country to the powder keg on which it sits. Its government appears convinced that the path of least resistance is to perpetually manage a crisis situation by tamping down with increased ferocity on Palestinians chafing under military occupation. It is easier for Israel to call for an F-16 fighter jet bomb run over Gaza or issue live-fire regulations against protesters in the West Bank than it is to reckon with the alternatives, all of which would entail some degree of withdrawal from its current hegemony over historic Palestine.

But the status quo is clearly unsustainable. In 2010, Israeli Jews became a minority of the total current inhabitants over whom Israel rules from the Jordan River to the Mediterranean Sea. The case for maintaining Israel as a "Jewish state" is even more precarious when Palestinian refugees and the global Palestinian diaspora are accounted for. Overall there are approximately two Palestinians worldwide for each Israeli Jew: the same ratio that existed on the eve of Israel's establishment still holds true today. Can a minority govern over a majority indigenous population in perpetuity? The history of decolonization in the developing world in the last century suggests not. Israel's current ability to rely upon the nearly unconditional diplomatic and military support of the world's superpower to maintain the status quo gives it a false comfort that it can continue to do so indeterminately.

If Israel's long-term goal is to maintain an exclusivist Jewish state with a Jewish majority, then its strategic interest dictates cutting loose the West Bank and Gaza Strip before history's powerful waves of inexorability wash over this improbable Zionist dream. But Israel is trapped in a box of its own making, wanting to have its cake and eat it too. This self-induced paralysis makes it unlikely that Israel will take any proactive measures to extricate itself from the ramifications of its colonization of Palestinian land. Israel has succeeded in undoing the 70-year-old UN recommendation to partition the land, in effect reconstituting the country as one geographical entity through its policies since 1967.

Israel's day of reckoning may come sooner than its leaders expect. If the Gaza Strip truly becomes uninhabitable, as predicted by the UN, in just three short years, then what will Israel do with the estimated 2.1 million Palestinians whose thirst must be slaked, whose hunger must be satiated, whose heads needs a roof to live under, trapped in a blockaded territory no longer capable of sustaining their daily necessities? Recent refugee crises and immigration flows suggest that borders, walls and fences cannot constrain desperate people on the move. Will Israel mow down hundreds of thousands of people attempting to flee their open-air

DID YOU KNOW?

That if a two-state resolution to the Israeli-Palestinian issue is not feasible, Americans by a margin of 65 to 24 percent prefer a "single democratic state in which Arabs and Jews are equals" to the continuation of Israel as a Jewish majority state "if it means that Palestinians will not have citizenship and full rights," according to a 2014 public opinion poll in *Foreign Policy*.

prison? What will Israel do if Palestinian refugees in the Gaza Strip simply decide to walk back *en masse* to the villages from which they were expelled in 1948, many of which are just a few miles away from Gaza?

Theoretically Israel could come to the realization that time is not on its side, uproot its illegal settlements in the West Bank and East Jerusalem, and offer Palestinians meaningful sovereignty in a state of their own on 22 percent of their historic homeland. Today the PLO would snatch that offer up in heartbeat even if it meant conceding that only a handful of Palestinian refugees would be able to exercise their right to return to their land in Israel. But with Palestinians under military occupation despairing of statehood—an October 2015 public opinion poll found two-thirds of Palestinians believe that the two-state solution is no longer practicable—that possibility may not exist tomorrow. And given the ideological trajectory of Israeli politics, there are no grounds for believing that its government will reverse course in this way.

With the two-state solution fading into obsolescence, the PLO's original political platform of establishing a secular, democratic state in all of historic Palestine re-presents itself as the only realistic alternative short of interminable bloodshed and unacceptable ethnic cleansing. Israeli Jews and Palestinians could coexist in equality in either a majoritarian one person, one vote constitutional arrangement (i.e. South Africa after apartheid) or in a binational framework (i.e. current day Belgium). Israel argues that this would necessitate the "destruction of the State of Israel."

Inasmuch as the State of Israel is predicated on maintaining itself as an exclusivist state privileging a minority population at the expense of the human and national rights of the indigenous majority population, such a development would indeed constitute a radical transformation of the current regime. But just such a transformation is needed if the Israeli-Palestinian issue is to be resolved and for Palestinians to achieve the freedom, justice and equality long denied to them.

## Sources:

Ambassador Martin Indyk, "Remarks on the Israeli-Palestinian Negotiations," US Department of State, May 8, 2014, available at https://2009-2017.state.gov/p/nea/rls/rm/225840.htm

"3 Years After Operation Cast Lead Justice has been Comprehensively Denied; PCHR Release 23 Narratives Documenting the Experience of Victims," Palestinian Centre for Human Rights, December 27, 2011, available at: http://www.pchrgaza.org/portal/en/index. php?option=com_content&view=article&id=7979:3-years-after-operation-cast-lead-justice-has-been-comprehensively-denied-pchr-release-23-narratives-documenting-the-experience-of-victims-&catid= 36:pchrpressreleases&Itemid=194

"B'Tselem's findings: Harm to civilians significantly higher in second half of Operation Pillar of Defense," B'Tselem—The Israeli Information Center for Human Rights in the Occupied Territories, May 8, 2013, available at: http://www.btselem.org/ press_releases/20130509_pillar_of_defense_report

"Gaza Emergency Situation Report," UN Office for the Coordination of Humanitarian Affairs, September 4, 2014, available at: http://www. ochaopt.org/documents/ocha_opt_sitrep_04_09_2014.pdf

Jodi Rudoren and Jeremy Ashkenas, "Netanyahu and the Settlements," New York Times, March 12, 2015, available at: http://www.nytimes.com/ interactive/2015/03/12/world/middleeast/netanyahu-west-bank-settlements-israel-election.html?_r=0

Gil Shefler, "'Jews now a minority between the River and the Sea'," *Jerusalem Post*, November 26, 2010, available at: http://www.jpost.com/National-News/Jews-now-a-minority-between-the-River-and-the-Sea

"Palestinian Public Opinion Poll No (57)," Palestinian Center for Policy and Survey Research, October 6, 2015, available at: http://www.pcpsr.org/en/node/621

"Water crisis in Gaza Strip: Over 90% of water un-potable," *B'Tselem*, February 6, 2014, available at http://www.btselem.org/gaza_strip/gaza_water_crisis

Shibley Telhami, ""America Has a Plan. And, No, It Isn't One That Israel Would Like,"

Foreign Policy, March 2, 2014, available at http://www.foreignpolicy.com/articles/2014/03/02/america_plan_israel_two_state

# Are Israeli Settlements Legal?

"Our basic conclusion is that from the point of view of international law, the classical laws of 'occupation' as set out in the relevant international conventions cannot be considered applicable to the unique and sui generis historic and legal circumstances of Israel's presence in Judea and Samaria [Israel's biblical term for the occupied Palestinian West Bank] spanning over decades. In addition, the provisions of the 1949 Fourth Geneva Convention, regarding transfer of populations, cannot be considered to be applicable and were never intended to apply to the type of settlement activity carried out by Israel in Judea and Samaria. Therefore, according to International law, Israelis have the legal right to settle in Judea and Samaria and the establishment of settlements cannot, in and of itself, be considered to be illegal."

—Israeli government-empaneled Levy Commission, July 2012

"The Israeli armed forces entered Gaza, the West Bank, Sinai and the Golan Heights in June 1967, in the course of an armed conflict. Those areas had not previously been part of Israel's sovereign territory nor otherwise under its administration. By reason of such entry of its armed forces, Israel established control and began to exercise authority over these territories; and under international law, Israel became a belligerent occupant of these territories... Article 49 of the Fourth Geneva Convention...provides, in paragraph 6: 'The Occupying Power shall not deport or transfer parts of its own civilian population into the territory it occupies'...While Israel may undertake, in the occupied territories, actions necessary to meet its military needs and to provide for orderly government during the occupation...the establishment of the civilian settlements in those territories is inconsistent with international law."

—Herbert Hansell, US State Department Legal Adviser, April 1978

## Sources:

"Conclusions and Recommendations," The Commission to Examine the Status of Building in Judea and Samaria, July 13, 2012, available at: http://unispal.un.org/UNISPAL.NSF/0/D9D07DCF58E781C585257A3A005956A6

"Concerning the Legality of Israeli Settlements in the Occupied Territories," Letter of the State Department Legal Advisor, Mr. Herbert J. Hansell, April 21, 1978, available at: http://unispal.un.org/UNISPAL.NSF/0/2DFED17DC7DFAE2A852563A9004C4055

# Israel: Democracy or Apartheid State?

Former President Jimmy Carter paid a dear price for suggesting that Israel may become an apartheid state in the future if it does not relinquish its occupation of the Palestinian West Bank. His 2006 book, *Palestine: Peace Not Apartheid,* ignited furious backlash. Carter was disinvited from speaking at the Democratic National Convention, condemned by senior Democratic members of Congress and treated like a pariah within his own political party.

Was Carter correct? Not exactly, at least in the opinion of two South Africans with peerless expertise on the subject. In 1961, South African Prime Minister Hendrik Verwoerd—the principal architect of twentieth-century apartheid in South Africa—stated: "The Jews took Israel from the Arabs after the Arabs had lived there for a thousand years. Israel, like South Africa, is an apartheid state." And from the polar opposite of the political spectrum, Archbishop Desmond Tutu, who won a Nobel Peace Prize for campaigning against apartheid, noted in an article entitled "Apartheid in the Holy Land" that his visit there "reminded me so much of what happened to us black people in South Africa."

The debate over whether Israel is an apartheid state too frequently revolves around comparisons to the former regime of racial segregation in South Africa. Israel, for example, points to the voting rights held by some Palestinians who live under its rule to differentiate itself from the apartheid experience in South Africa, in which no black South Africans were enfranchised. No two historical situations are exactly analogous, and whether Israel is similar to or different from the former regime in South Africa is immaterial to the discussion.

What matters is whether Israel's policies toward Palestinians meet the international definition of apartheid, a crime against humanity according to the 1973 UN Convention on the Suppression and Punishment of the Crime of Apartheid. This convention cites "legislative measures...calculated to prevent a racial group...from participation in the political, social, economic and cultural life of the country" as constituting apartheid. Specific examples of apartheid include denying groups "basic human rights and freedoms," "the right to leave and to return to their country, the right to a nationality," and "the right to freedom of peaceful assembly and association."

According to Israel's laws and military orders, its policies toward Palestinians incontrovertibly constitute acts of apartheid. Laws which establish Israel's national flag and state seal as Jewish religious symbols are just two of dozens which discriminate against Palestinian citizens, rendering them second-class citizens of a country born on the ruins of their society. While Israel denies Palestinian refugees their right of return, it confers automatic citizenship on any Jewish person who immigrates under the Law of Return. And Palestinians have been banned from protesting Israel's military occupation of the West Bank and Gaza Strip since its inception.

Democracy is not synonymous with voting rights, and the right of only selected groups to vote clearly disqualifies a country from being considered a democracy. It is the commitment to and implementation of the principle of equality under the law that confers a state's democratic bona fides. Until Israel dismantles its separate and unequal policies privileging Israeli Jews and discriminating against Palestinians, its pretension to democracy will remain threadbare.

Not only do Israel's discriminatory policies toward Palestinians disqualify it from being considered a democracy that bestows equal rights on all the people over whom it rules. In recent years, the veneer of Israeli parliamentary democratic procedures and rights to freedom of expression, which have previously served the county so well in its appeals toward inclusion among the family of democratic nations, has worn thin. As the illusions of the "peace process" have faded and Israel's grasp on the Palestinian West Bank and Gaza Strip appears more permanent than ever, Israel's international isolation has risen concomitantly, precipitating the Israeli parliament to enact a rash of legislation designed to quash political speech.

For example, in 2011, the Knesset passed a law called "Preventing Harm to the State of Israel by Means of Boycott." The law opens the door for corporations to sue Israeli citizens (Jewish or Palestinian) who call for boycotts, including limited boycotts of goods produced in Israeli settlements. If a company can prove that its bottom line was negatively affected by the words or actions of someone calling for a boycott of its product, then that individual or organization could be sued and made to pay compensation.

In addition, the law imposes heavy-handed sanctions on Israeli organizations or corporations supporting calls to boycott. Nongovernmental organizations (NGOs) can be stripped of their tax-exempt status and corporations can be disqualified from receiving government contracts. As intended, the law has had a drastic chilling effect on the willingness of Israeli individuals, organizations, and companies to advocate for boycotts and has succeeded in helping to curtail the boundaries of what is considered acceptable discourse in Israeli society.

Another law approved by the Knesset in 2016, known informally as "the NGO Law," illustrates the shrinking of civil society space open to Israelis to question their government's policies. The law was narrowly written to target organizations receiving funding from foreign governmental sources or from the United Nations, which many Israeli human rights organizations admittedly accept due to the difficulty of raising money domestically and from private foreign donors to support their work. The law requires NGOs receiving a majority of their funding from these sources to disclose the fact in all of their publications. The original version of the bill contained even more draconian stipulations, such as requiring these NGOs to wear special identification tags while lobbying in the Knesset.

Although this provision was stripped from the final version of the bill, the law remains problematic because it is designed to stigmatize and discredit Israeli organizations doing valuable work to document the country's human rights violations. The discriminatory intent of the law is clear because it does not impose the same requirements on Israeli NGOs receiving the bulk of their funding from private foreign donors. Not coincidentally, many organizations promoting right-wing causes, such as Israel's colonization of Palestinian land and even the replacement of Muslim holy sites in Jerusalem with a rebuilt Jewish temple, are funded primarily or solely by foreign tax-exempt organizations.

In 2016, the Knesset also passed a basic law, a type of legislation which has a quasi-constitutional status, facilitating the impeachment of elected members of parliament. While democracies should have procedures for removing elected officials who have behaved un-ethically or illegally, they cannot legitimately impeach them for the content of their political speech in parliament, which is what Israel's law strives to do. The law enables a member of parliament to be removed by a three-quarters vote if that person "encourages terror-ism or incitement to violence," vague charges which Israeli Jewish members of Knesset regularly hurl at Palestinian-Israeli members of Knesset for such things as attending conferences in countries with which Israel is in a state of war, opposing Israeli military operations, participating in humanitarian flotillas to break Israel's blockade of the Gaza Strip or asserting that Palestinians are entitled to resist Israeli military occupation under international law.

A coalition of Palestinian political parties is currently the third-largest bloc in Israel's parliament, and the increasing political clout of Palestinian citizens of Israel and their vision for a secular state with equal rights for all of its citizens presents a fundamental challenge to the Zionist ideology of a state built to privilege Jewish people. This law could be wielded in the future to expel members of these Palestinian political parties, and the Association for Civil Rights in Israel warns that it is "liable to cause the permanent exclusion of entire sectors from the political system."

While this law has not yet been employed to enforce ideological conformity in Israel's parliament, another law passed by the Knesset in 2017 applying to foreigners clearly shows the trajectory in which Israel is heading: excluding entire groups of people based on their political beliefs. Israel has long denied entry to foreigners it deems to have hostile political opinions, often engaging in invasive searches of email and social media to ferret out undesirables. This often arbitrary practice was systematized in the "Entry to Israel Bill," which denies outright the ability of foreigners to get visas or work permits if they support boycotting Israel, or even just Israeli settlement products. As Israel controls entry to and exit from the West Bank and Gaza Strip as well, this means that foreigners holding this view who desire to visit or work in Occupied Palestinian Territory will be prohibited from doing so.

A country which establishes one set of laws for a privileged class and another set designed for those whose existence is unwanted cannot be considered democratic. And a country which is increasingly constricting the political space available to challenge this discriminatory order demonstrates its fragility and tenuousness.

## Sources:

Chris McGreal, "Worlds Apart," *The Guardian*, February 6, 2006, available at: http://www.theguardian.com/world/2006/feb/06/southafrica.israel

Desmond Tutu, "Apartheid in the Holy Land, *The Guardian*, April 28, 2002, available at: http://www.theguardian.com/world/2002/apr/29/comment

International Convention on the Suppression and Punishment of the Crime of Apartheid, adopted by the UN General Assembly, November 30, 1973, available at: https://treaties.un.org/doc/Publication/UNTS/Volume%201015/volume-1015-I-14861-English.pdf

"Update: Anti-Democratic Legislation Initiatives," Association for Civil Rights in Israel, August 2, 2012, available at: http://www.acri.org.il/en/2012/08/02/update-anti-democratic-legislation-initiatives/

"Overview of Anti-Democratic Legislation in the 20th Knesset," Association for Civil Rights in Israel, March 2017, available at: http://www.acri.org.il/en/wp-content/uploads/2016/09/Overview-of-Anti-Democratic-Legislation-March-2017-1.pdf

# Parting Thought

"For if life had taught her anything, it was that healing and peace can begin only with acknowledgment of wrongs committed."

—Susan Abulhawa, *Mornings in Jenin*

# Image credits

PAGE VIII & 5   Photographs by Josh Ruebner.

PAGE 18 & 24   Photographs courtesy of Library of Congress, World War I and the British Mandate in Palestine collection.

PAGE 28   Jerusalem seen from the Mount of Olives |Flickr/twiga_swala. Creative Commons.

PAGES 40 & 41   Photographs courtesy of Institute for Palestine Studies. Used with permission.

PAGE 58   White House photograph | Vince Musi. Courtesy of the National Archives.

PAGE 60   Map courtesy of United Nations Office for the Coordination of Humanitarian Affairs, occupied Palestinian territory.

PAGE 68   Photograph courtesy of United States Department of State.

PAGE 70   White House photograph | Shealah Craighead.

# Index

## YOUNG PALESTINIANS SPEAK
### LIVING UNDER OCCUPATION
**Anthony Robinson and Annemarie Young**
8" x 9" • 144 pages • full-color
ISBN 978-1-56656-015-3 • hardback • $19.99

"Many books have been written about Palestine but few from the perspective of young adults… This book is unique…. It will move hearts and minds and will educate a new generation of English readers to the tragedy of Palestine and what Palestinians living under occupation have to endure."

—Raja Shehadeh, author of the
Orwell Prize-Winning *Palestinian Walks*

"Children, teens, and 20-somethings, from all over Gaza Strip and the West Bank, speak in their own voices about their daily experiences of living under occupation… What readers will discover is that these young Palestinians want the same things young people want everywhere: a stable family life, the freedom to move about their country, and a safe and secure space in which to grow up… A poignant, powerful, and insightful collection of voices seldom heard. (photos, maps, timeline, references) (Nonfiction. 12-18)"

—*Kirkus Reviews*

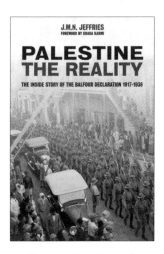

## PALESTINE THE REALITY
## THE INSIDE STORY OF THE BALFOUR DECLARATION
## 1917–1938
## J.M.N. Jeffries
6" x 9" • 800 pages • ISBN 978-1-56656-024-5 • paperback • $30

The Balfour Declaration of 1917 is a document that profoundly affected the Middle East. *Palestine: The Reality* is an expertly researched inside story of the Declaration. It is also a vivid and personal account in which J.M.N. Jeffries exposes the real authors and progenitors of the Balfour Declaration, along with their personal stories, motives, conspiracies, and political aims. The author also details the other international players who were involved in the creation of the "Balfour" document, and offers a clearsighted perspective on the broken agreements with Britain's Arab allies that enabled the Declaration and dispossessed the Palestinian Arabs of their homeland.

**Joseph Mary Nagle Jeffries** (1880-1960) was a war, foreign, and political correspondent for *The Daily Mail* in London from 1914 until the late 1930s.

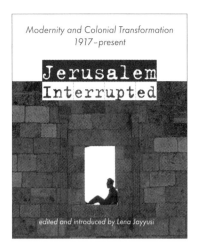

## JERUSALEM INTERRUPTED
### MODERNITY AND COLONIAL TRANSFORMATION
### 1917–PRESENT
**edited and introduced by Lena Jayyusi**
7.5" x 9.25" • 552 pages • color photos throughout
ISBN 978-1-56656-787-9 • paperback • $60

This groundbreaking collection of essays brings together distinguished scholars and writers and follows the history of Jerusalem from the culturally diverse Mandate period through its transformation into a predominantly Jewish city. Contributors include: Lena Jayyusi, Issam Nassar, Samia A. Halaby, Elias Sahhab, Andrea Stanton, Makram Khoury-Machool, Sandy Sufian, Awad Halabi, Ellen L. Fleischmann, Widad Kawar, Rochelle Davis, Subhi Ghosheh, Mohammad Ghosheh, Tom Abowd, Nadia Abu El-Haj, Michael Dumper, Nahed Awwad, Ahmad J. Azem, Nasser Abourahme.

"The scope is wide: archaeology, art and handcrafts, photography, music, health, memoir, festivals, and historical incidents. ... Especially interesting are essays on the political mobilization of women during the British Mandate period and historical photos, e.g., those of the once-active Jerusalem airport in the occupied West Bank. Summing Up: Recommended. Most levels/libraries."
—CHOICE

# SEEKING PALESTINE
## NEW PALESTINIAN WRITING ON EXILE AND HOME
### edited by Penny Johnson and Raja Shehadeh
6" x 9" • 202 pages • ISBN 9781566569064 • paperback • $16

How do Palestinians live, imagine, and reflect on home and exile in this period of a stateless and transitory Palestine and a sharp escalation in Israeli state violence and accompanying Palestinian oppression? How can exile and home be written? In this volume of new writing, fifteen innovative and outstanding Palestinian writers—essayists, poets, novelists, critics, artists, and memoirists—respond with their reflections, experiences, memories, and polemics. Their contributions—poignant, humorous, intimate, reflective, intensely political—make for an offering that is remarkable for the candor and grace with which it explores the many individual and collective experiences of waiting for, living for, and seeking Palestine.

Contributors include: Lila Abu-Lughod, Susan Abulhawa, Suad Amiry, Rana Barakat, Mourid Barghouti, Beshara Doumani, Sharif S. Elmusa, Rema Hammami, Mischa Hiller, Emily Jacir, Penny Johnson, Fady Joudah, Jean Said Makdisi, Karma Nabulsi, Raeda Sa'adeh, Raja Shehadeh, Adania Shibli.